...quillity, provide for the common defense, promote the general Welfare, and secure the...

...ity, provide for the common defense, promote the general Welfare, and secure the Blessings of

Article. I. Section. I. All legislative Powers herein granted shall be vested in a Congress of the

...le. I. Section. 1. All legislative Powers herein granted shall be vested in a Congress of the

...tives shall be composed of Members chosen every second Year by the People of the several States,

...s shall be composed of Members chosen every second Year by the People of the several States,

...e State Legislature. No Person shall be a Representative who shall not have attained to the

...State Legislature. No Person shall be a Representative who shall not have attained to the

...Inhabitant of that State in which he shall be chosen. Representatives and direct Taxes shall be

...Inhabitant of that State in which he shall be chosen. Representatives and direct Taxes shall be

...which shall be determined by adding to the whole Number of free Persons, including those bound

...which shall be determined by adding to the whole Number of free Persons, including those bound

...ndment XIV). The actual Enumeration shall be made within three Years after the first Meeting

...nt XIV]. The actual Enumeration shall be made within three Years after the first Meeting

...Law direct. The Number of Representatives shall not exceed one for every thirty Thousand, but

...Law direct. The Number of Representatives shall not exceed one for every thirty Thousand, but

...mpshire shall be entitled to choose three, Massachusetts eight, Rhode-Island and Providence

...ire shall be entitled to choose three, Massachusetts eight, Rhode-Island and Providence

...six, Virginia ten, North Carolina five, South Carolina five, and Georgia three.

...inia ten, North Carolina five, South Carolina five, and Georgia three.

To: Jesse —
A future Thurgood Marshall!

Juan Williams
11:30·00
Goshen, Ind.

Thurgood Marshall:

TIME-LIFE
History Makers

Freedom's Defender

Letter to the Reader

Dear Reader,

This book tells the story of Thurgood Marshall, whose work as a lawyer and Supreme Court justice has touched the lives of all Americans. When he died in 1993, Justice Marshall left an important legacy. He helped to change the laws that denied equal rights to women and minorities.

In this book, different terms are used to identify African Americans. When Justice Marshall was a young man, African Americans usually were referred to as "Negroes" or "colored." During the 1960s, African Americans began to refer to themselves as "blacks." And since the 1980s, most Americans whose ancestors came from the African continent have preferred the term "African American." For most of his life, Justice Marshall preferred the word "Negro."

In this biography, the term "nigger" appears in some quotations. When this term is used, it merely recites the words of the speaker. It is, however, an insulting and harmful word that does not describe or define any person or group.

Leland Ware
Author

Thurgood Marshall:
Freedom's Defender

Leland Ware

Time Life Education   Alexandria, Virginia

Key Events in Thurgood Marshall's Life

	Key Events Around the World

Thurgood Marshall's Life		Around the World
1908 — Thurgood Marshall is born in Baltimore, Maryland, on July 2.	**1908-1921**	1914 — World War I begins with an assassination in Austria-Hungary.
1925 — Thurgood Marshall enrolls at Lincoln University in Oxford, Pennsylvania.	**1921-1930**	1929 — The U.S. stock market crashes and sets off a period called the Great Depression.
1933 — Thurgood receives a law degree from Howard University in Washington, D.C.	**1930-1933**	1932 — Franklin Roosevelt is elected president and promises a "new deal" for the country.
1935 — Thurgood, with his mentor, Charles Houston, wins his first major civil-rights case: *Murray v. Maryland*.	**1933-1935**	1934 — The Apollo Theatre opens in Harlem.
1936 — Thurgood and his wife, Vivian, move to New York so he can become special counsel for the National Association for the Advancement of Colored People (NAACP).	**1935-1946**	1939 — World War II begins when Germany invades Poland.
1948 — As chief counsel for the NAACP, Thurgood leads the appeal on the restrictive-covenants cases before the Supreme Court.	**1946-1948**	1947 — Jackie Robinson signs a contract to play major league baseball with the Brooklyn Dodgers, breaking the "color barrier."
1948 — Thurgood begins arguing cases that challenge segregation in state universities: *Sipuel, McLaurin,* and *Sweatt*.	**1948-1950**	1948 — President Truman signs an order that ends segregation in the military and in government jobs.
1950 — Thurgood is deeply affected by the death of his longtime friend and mentor, Charles Houston.	**1950-1952**	1950 — Ralph Bunche, ambassador to the United Nations, is the first African American to win the Nobel Peace Prize.
1954 — Thurgood persuades the Supreme Court to declare segregation in public schools unconstitutional in *Brown v. Board of Education*.	**1952-1955**	1955 — Rosa Parks refuses to give up her seat to a white man on a Montgomery, Alabama, public bus, triggering the Montgomery bus boycott.
1965 — President Johnson appoints Thurgood Marshall solicitor general, and two years later nominates him to the Supreme Court.	**1955-1967**	1957 — President Eisenhower orders federal troops to escort black students to Central High School in Little Rock, Arkansas, following court-ordered integration.
1991 — Thurgood Marshall retires from the Supreme Court and dies two years later, at the age of 84.	**1967-1993**	1989 — African American Colin L. Powell is appointed chairman of the Joint Chiefs of Staff by President Bush.

Thurgood Marshall: Freedom's Defender

A *Spirited* Child

Chapter 1

1908 - 1921

Key Events in Thurgood Marshall's Life

Key Events Around the World

1905

1908

William and Norma Marshall welcome their second child, Thoroughgood, into the world.

King Leopold of Belgium takes control of the country in Africa known as the Congo.

1909

1910

The Marshall family moves to the Harlem section of New York City, and Norma Marshall attends Columbia University.

The National Association for the Advancement of Colored People (NAACP) is founded in New York City.

The NAACP begins publishing its journal, *Crisis*.

1914

The Marshalls return to their hometown of Baltimore, Maryland.

1915

The modern Ku Klux Klan is organized in the state of Georgia.

Thoroughgood Marshall enters second grade and changes his name to Thurgood.

1918

President Woodrow Wilson proposes a League of Nations as part of his Fourteen Points for the treaty to end World War I.

1919

1920

Race riots break out in 25 American cities.

1921

Thurgood enters Baltimore's only high school for African-American students, Frederick Douglass High School.

A "renaissance" of artistic expression begins in Harlem, the largest African-American urban center in the world. Women get the vote.

1925

Young Thurgood Marshall came home from school one day and asked his father about a word he had just heard. Two boys were fighting in the schoolyard, he told his father, and one of the boys had called the other a "nigger." Thurgood wanted to know what the word meant. His father's answer would stay with him for the rest of his life. It also would begin to change him in a way that would affect the lives of millions of Americans.

William Marshall carefully explained to his son that it was the worst word anyone could use against an African American. It was a word of hate. It was a word of ignorance. It was a word that white people used to put down black people. "Thurgood," his father said sternly, "anyone calls you a 'nigger,' you not only got my permission to fight him—you got my *orders* to fight him!"

That's exactly what happened, a few years later, when Thurgood was 15. By then he had a part-time job delivering hats. Each day after school, Thurgood rushed over to the clothing store, near his home in Baltimore, Maryland. There he picked up a load of hatboxes to deliver to the store's customers.

One afternoon, Thurgood set out with a large load of boxes. The boxes were piled up so high that he could hardly see where he was going. He managed to get to the streetcar stop, just outside the store, where several people were waiting. When the streetcar arrived, Thurgood rushed to climb aboard. Suddenly he felt a strong hand pull him back by his shirt collar.

An angry voice said, "Nigger, don't you push in front of white people." As soon as Thurgood heard that word, he recalled his father's lecture. A tall lad for his age, he dropped the hatboxes and tore in to the

Children playing in an alley in Baltimore, Maryland.

Streetcars on Howard Street in Baltimore, around 1914.

man who had pulled him back. The two of them ended up on the pavement, wrestling and punching. A crowd quickly gathered to watch the fight, and the commotion drew the attention of a policeman. But instead of asking what happened, the policeman arrested Thurgood—and not the other man.

When Thurgood called the hat store owner from the police station, his boss came quickly to bail him out. He listened to Thurgood's story and then persuaded the police to drop the charges. As they walked back to the store, the owner asked Thurgood if the man really had called him that hateful name. "Yes sir, he sure did," Thurgood replied. He also apologized for ruining the pile of hats, but his boss simply said that Thurgood had done the right thing. His boss was Jewish. He had been called some awful names during his lifetime, too, so he knew how it felt.

Use the Law, Not Fists

Thurgood Marshall didn't get into many fights like that. For one thing, just about anywhere in America at that time, standing up to a white man usually meant time in jail, or worse. But mostly, Thurgood didn't like fighting that much. He preferred debates, telling stories, and having a good time. He had lots of good times at parties with his friends. He also loved telling stories to just about anyone who would listen. But his favorite place for debates was in the courtroom. He spent most of his adult life in courtrooms, first as a lawyer, then as a judge. Using the law instead of his fists, Thurgood Marshall helped to win one of the biggest legal battles in the history of the United States—the battle to end segregation. He also helped to make America a better place for

Bail:

To pay money to release an arrested person from jail until he or she has to appear in court.

Supreme Court justice Thurgood Marshall.

Segregation:

Separating people because of their race, class, or ethnic origin.

everyone—no matter what their gender, skin color, religion, or ethnic background might be. He made it easier for people to become whatever they wanted to be.

Independent Spirits

One of Thurgood's favorite stories was about one of his own ancestors:

Way back before the Civil War, this rich man from Maryland went to the Congo (in Africa) on a hunting expedition or something. The whole time that he was there, this little black boy trailed him around. So when they got ready to come back to this country, they just picked him up and brought him along.

The years passed, and he grew up, and, boy, he grew up into one *mean* man! *One day his owner came to him and said, "You're so evil I've got to get rid of you. But I in good conscience can't sell you to another white person. So I'm telling you what I'll do—if you get out of town, I'll give you your freedom."*

Well, [the man] never said a word—just . . . walked off the place, settled down a couple miles away, raised his family and lived there till the day he died. And nobody ever laid a hand on him.

This story, like most good tales, has parts that are made up and parts that are true. That was the way Thurgood loved to tell them—"swapping lies," as he would say. But many of his family stories were completely true. Thurgood's family was full of independent spirits, people who worked

Ancestors:
People from whom a person is descended, especially those from a generation older than grandparents.

Engraving courtesy of Library of Congress, LC-USZ62-38798.

A young escaped slave.

Enslaved:

Forced to work for someone as a slave.

Free blacks:

African Americans who were freed from slavery before the end of the Civil War or who never were enslaved.

Black cavalrymen known as buffalo soldiers, in 1895.

Navy seamen in the late 1800s, around the time Thurgood's grandfather served in the U.S. Navy.

and fought hard for themselves and their children. One of these was Thorney Good Marshall, Thurgood's grandfather.

Thorney Marshall had been enslaved as a child. During the Civil War, he escaped to Baltimore, Maryland. There, Thorney found work, made friends, and blended into the city's large population of free blacks. After the war, he joined the U.S. Army and became a buffalo soldier—the name Native Americans gave to black soldiers. Partly it was because they were tough, like buffaloes. Also, many of them wore coats made from buffalo hides in cold weather.

Thorney needed to be tough for his army job. He guarded payroll shipments between Brownsville, Texas, and the army's forts along the Rio Grande. But he had no need for buffalo hides. Brownsville, the southernmost town in Texas, has a hot climate. The land is marshy and full of mosquitoes. After several years, Thorney became ill and had to leave the army. He returned to Baltimore, where he was hospitalized and nearly died. When he recovered, he met a young woman named Annie Robinson. They fell in love, got married, and opened a grocery store in the western part of the city. Thorney and Annie had seven children, including William Canfield Marshall. "Willie," as they called him, would become Thurgood Marshall's father.

A Family of Achievers

Thurgood's other grandfather was an early champion of equal rights for African Americans. Isaiah Olive Branch Williams served in the Union navy in the Civil War. After the war, he stayed three more years, sailing up and down the Pacific coast of South America. Finally, he returned to his hometown of Baltimore. Like Thorney Good Marshall, Isaiah Williams got married and opened a grocery store. Both men lived in the same West Baltimore neighborhood.

Over the years, Isaiah became a respected figure in his community. He also was a powerful role model for his children and grandchildren. In the summer of 1875, the police were called to break up a loud party near Isaiah's store. A fight broke out, and a white police officer shot a black man. Isaiah organized a protest against the shooting. He gave a stirring speech, calling for "the same protection in life, liberty, and the pursuit of happiness which white men enjoy as a right." Isaiah's efforts led to jail time for the white policeman on a manslaughter charge.

Isaiah's wife, Mary Fossett, had learned to read by the time she was 12. This was a major accomplishment for an African-American girl at the time. She taught at a private school for black children but stopped when she and Isaiah began to have their own children—six in all. Isaiah named one daughter for an Italian opera, *Norma*. He had seen it during his navy days, in the town of Arica, Chile. Norma Arica Williams would become Thurgood Marshall's mother.

Norma Williams grew up to be a teacher, like her mother and her older sister. She attended Coppin State College, in Baltimore. Later, she earned a master's degree from Columbia University, in New York City. She met William Marshall while she was in college, and they were married just before she graduated. Their first son, William Aubrey, was born in 1904. Thurgood arrived four years later, on July 2, 1908.

Lexington Market in Baltimore, Maryland, around 1910.

Manslaughter:
Killing someone without intending to do so, a lesser crime than murder.

A turn-of-the-century grocery store in Baltimore, Maryland, similar to those owned by Thurgood's grandfathers.

Thurgood Marshall at age one.

Birth certificate:

An official record of a person's date and place of birth.

Integrated:

A mix of races, genders, and ethnic groups, to whom services are equally available.

Baltimore's Division Street in August 1939.

A "Smart Little Fella"

Although Thurgood's name resembles his grandfather's—Thorney Good—his parents actually named him for his father's brother, *Thoroughgood* Marshall. That was his name until he was about seven years old. Then, young Thurgood showed his own independent spirit for the first time. He decided to change his name.

"By the time I got to second grade," he explained, "I got tired of spelling all that and shortened it." He was so determined about it that he even persuaded his parents to change his name on his birth certificate. Thurgood's aunts and uncles nicknamed him Goody. "He was always a smart, alert little fella," one aunt recalled. "He was full of life and laughter." A family friend noted something else about him:

> *I can still see Thurgood coming down Division Street. He'd [have] both hands dug way into his pockets and be kicking a stone in front of him, [on his way] to visit his grandparents at their big grocery store on the corner. He was in a deep study, that boy, and it was plain something was going on inside of him.*

His independent streak also enabled him to get his first job when he was seven. At the time, Division Street in Baltimore was an integrated neighborhood, something almost unknown in America at the time. Black families lived among white families of many origins—Russians, Italians, Germans, and others. Thurgood delivered groceries for a Jewish store owner who lived a few doors away. He earned 10 cents a day pulling bags of groceries around the neighborhood in a little wagon. Thurgood grew up in a community where blacks and whites lived together peacefully. His best childhood friend was the store owner's son.

One of the Roughnecks

It wasn't a perfect peace, however. Sometimes, he and the neighborhood boys got into fights. Once, when he was a lawyer, he arrived in a courtroom to begin a case, and an assistant state's attorney approached him:

> *He mentioned the fact that I should remember him. And I said I was sorry, I didn't. He said, "Well, if you don't remember me, I remember you." [Then] he showed me a little scar . . . on his forehead, which I remembered that I gave him, in a little fight we had.*

Most of the time, however, Thurgood and the neighborhood boys just played together—even if their play was a little rough:

> *We lived on a respectable street, but behind us were back alleys where roughnecks and the tough kids hung out. When it was time for dinner, my mother would go to the front door to call my older brother. Then she'd go to the back door and call me.*

Actually, Thurgood got into trouble more at school than at home—not for fighting, but for talking, laughing, and teasing the girls in his class. His teachers often made him sit in the front row, where they could watch him more closely. Once, when he was in high school, Thurgood's principal sent him to the basement with a copy of the U.S. Constitution

Boys playing in a city alley, around 1935.

State's attorney:

A lawyer appointed to represent a state government in a court trial.

Frederick Douglass High School, the segregated high school Thurgood Marshall attended in Baltimore, Maryland.

Baltimore's Druid Hill Avenue, today.

Colored:

A once common word used to describe people of color.

William Marshall worked as a dining car waiter, similar to the one shown here.

and ordered him to memorize a section of it. As he recalled later, "Before I left that school, I knew the entire Constitution by heart."

Family Influences

Eventually, the Marshall family moved into a large brick row house on Druid Hill Avenue. It was where many in Baltimore's black middle class lived—doctors, lawyers, business owners, teachers, and other professionals.

While Norma Marshall taught in one of segregated Baltimore's colored elementary schools, William worked as a dining car waiter for the Baltimore & Ohio Railroad. It was a good job, especially for an African American, because it could be exciting. Railroad workers got to see more of the country than most Americans. Cars were rare and owned mostly by the rich, and airplanes had just been invented. Many people never left the communities where they were born.

William was paid well, mostly from the tips he collected from wealthy travelers. The only trouble was that while Thurgood and his brother, William Aubrey—now known as Aubrey—were young, their father often was away from home. Even so, he was a strong influence on his sons. William had dropped out of school at an early age. He warned his boys not to make the same mistake. Norma had studied hard to get her degrees, and she was proud of her achievements. Both parents were determined to provide Thurgood and Aubrey with the best education they could afford. They saw education as the key to success.

A *Growing* Awareness

Chapter 2   1921 - 1930

Key Events in Thurgood Marshall's Life

	Key Events Around the World
	1920
	1921 The Senate rejects U.S. membership in the League of Nations.
	1922
	African-American actor Paul Robeson begins his career on Broadway.
Thurgood graduates from Frederick Douglass High School and enrolls at Lincoln University.	**1925** A. Philip Randolph organizes the Brotherhood of Sleeping Car Porters.
	1926
	Mordecai Johnson becomes the first African-American president of Howard University.
	1927
	Charles Lindbergh is the first to fly solo from New York to Paris. Duke Ellington first appears at Harlem's Cotton Club.
Thurgood marries Vivian Burey.	**1929**
	1930 The International Ladies' Garment Workers' Union organizes African-American workers.
	African-American pitcher Josh Gibson begins his baseball career with the Pittsburgh Homestead Grays.
	1935
	1940

William and Norma Marshall had big plans for their sons. They wanted Aubrey to become a doctor and Thurgood to become a dentist. There were few African Americans in either profession in the first half of the 20th century. During that time, with few exceptions there were two very separate Americas. One was white and one was black.

Thurgood began to learn about this separation when he was a child. As he grew older, he experienced the shame felt by many African Americans living under segregation. One incident was especially painful. One day, he was in downtown Baltimore when he realized he needed to use the bathroom. He looked in several places, but the only restrooms he found had signs that read: "Whites Only." In a near panic, Thurgood hopped on a streetcar and headed for home. He made it only to his front steps. It was an experience he would never forget.

Separate Worlds

Insults and shame were part of everyday life for most African Americans at that time. "Whites only" signs could be seen in many restaurants, department stores, hotels, and hospitals. Even water fountains were segregated. In some ways, segregation was as cruel as the system of slavery that it had replaced. Segregation reminded black people that whites thought they were inferior—fit only to be servants in their homes, janitors in their buildings, or waiters in their restaurants and railroad dining cars.

The list of insults was long and shameful. Black people were kept out of white neighborhoods. In many areas, they could not serve on juries.

A sign used to separate "colored" people and "white" people.

Top: A black man drinks at a segregated water cooler in a streetcar terminal.

A black man walks up to the balcony in a segregated movie theater in 1939.

An all-black school in rural Georgia in 1941.

They had to use tax forms that were a different color than those for whites. They had to use separate teller windows at banks. In office buildings, most elevators were for "whites only," so they had to walk up the steps. Movie theaters did not allow them to use the front door or to sit in the main section, so they entered through the side door and sat in the balcony, far from the movie screen. They also sat in separate cars on trains. When cities began to use buses, blacks were forced to ride in the back and give up their seats if white people were standing.

In the South, the Jim Crow laws that supported these unfair conditions also kept many blacks from voting. Jim Crow was the name of a character in a 19th-century minstrel show. A white man blackened his face and acted ignorant and foolish. The laws became known by the character's name.

Black children were forced to attend separate schools. The buildings usually were old, poorly maintained, and did not have enough classrooms or space for gyms and libraries. "Colored" schools had fewer books and supplies than schools for white children. Thurgood and his brother attended Frederick Douglass High School in Baltimore. It was so overcrowded that half of the students went to classes in the morning, and the other half went in the afternoon. The city built a new high school in 1926, the year after Thurgood graduated. Plans for the new school included a swimming pool, but Baltimore's superintendent of schools stopped its construction. As Thurgood later recalled, the superintendent said black students "didn't deserve swimming pools."

Separate but Equal?

African Americans were nearly powerless to fight this unfair treatment. The major reason was that Jim Crow laws had the support of the U.S. Supreme Court.

In 1896, the Supreme Court decided a case called *Plessy v. Ferguson.* The case arose from an incident in Louisiana. Homer Plessy was a person of mixed race. One of his great-grandparents was black, and the other seven were white. After Plessy boarded a train in New Orleans, a conductor ordered him to move to a car that was reserved for black passengers. Plessy refused to obey and was arrested under the segregation laws. A person was considered black if he or she had as little as "one drop of black blood."

Plessy sued the railroad company. His lawyer argued that the Louisiana law violated the 14th Amendment to the U.S. Constitution. That amendment guarantees equal protection under the law. But Louisiana's laws—as well as the laws of many other states—required "equal but separate accommodations for the white and for the colored races." Anyone who violated those laws could be sent to prison.

Plessy lost his case in Louisiana, so he appealed the case to the Supreme Court. In one of the most shameful decisions in American history, the Court rejected his appeal. Eight of the nine judges voted that the segregation laws did not violate the 14th Amendment, as long as the state provided equal facilities for both races. Justice John Marshall Harlan wrote a powerful dissenting opinion, however. He argued that segregation laws were unfair because they assumed that black people

An advertisement for the railroad company sued by Homer Plessy.

Conductor:
A railroad worker who supervises the train crew and collects fares from passengers.

Sued:
Took legal action against someone in court.

Accommodations:
A place to receive services, such as dining, transportation, or lodging.

Dissenting opinion:
A judge's formal written disagreement with the decision of the majority of judges hearing a case.

Justice John Marshall Harlan.

Thurgood Marshall also worked as a waiter on the railroads, wearing a uniform like the one shown above.

were inferior to whites. There could be no equality in segregation. According to Justice Harlan, "our Constitution is color blind, and [it] neither knows nor tolerates classes among citizens."

The Supreme Court's *Plessy* decision gave segregation legal approval from the highest court in the land. As long as the ruling was in place, only white people could enjoy the freedoms promised by the U.S. Constitution. Segregation would be difficult to overturn!

Swallowing Pride

As Thurgood neared the end of his high-school career, he worked hard to earn enough money for college. Although he never accepted the ideas of segregation—that he was inferior to white people—he had to be practical about his goals. Sometimes that meant swallowing his pride. In early 1925, he was offered a job as a dining car waiter on the Baltimore & Ohio Railroad, where his father had worked. His black supervisor gave him a choice:

> *The first day, I was given a white coat and dark pants [a waiter's uniform]. But the pants were too short. So I told the supervisor I needed longer pants. He said, "Boy, we can get a man to fit the pants a lot easier than we can get pants to fit the man. Why don't you just scrunch down in 'em a little?" So, I scrunched.*

Thurgood didn't argue with his supervisor, because he needed the job. His father had become ill and couldn't work. His parents already were struggling to put his brother, Aubrey, through college, and they were determined to send Thurgood as well.

If the Marshalls could raise $300 more, Thurgood could attend college in the fall. He wasn't the top student in his high school, but he had maintained a strong B average. He had never failed a class, had never been late to school, and had been absent only one day. He had finished his schoolwork several months early to begin his job in the spring instead of the summer. The extra time meant he could earn extra money. So he "scrunched" into that waiter's uniform and earned the money he needed for college.

Thurgood Marshall's graduation photo from Frederick Douglass High School in 1925.

The Loudest Voice

Thurgood Marshall was best known in high school for his success on the debating team. He was so good that he was elected captain when he was only a freshman. Years later he explained that his debating style grew out of the many arguments he had with his brother and father:

> We'd argue about everything . . . five out of seven nights at the dinner table. When we were away . . . and we would come back, . . . I remember a neighbor of ours would tell her husband, "Ah, the [Marshall] boys are home!"

William Marshall strongly influenced Thurgood in another way—he took his son to see dramatic trials in the city's courtrooms. William would observe the techniques that lawyers used in their arguments, then use them on his son at dinner. Thurgood's interest in the law was sparked by these field trips with his father.

The entrance to Lincoln University, in Oxford, Pennsylvania.

Poet and playwright Langston Hughes in 1942.

Thurgood also had a mentor—his high-school history teacher, Gough McDaniels, who coached the debating team. McDaniels often pushed Thurgood to do extra research for his debates. The work paid off. His high-school debating team was one of the best in Baltimore.

Thurgood carried his debating skills to college when he entered Lincoln University in the fall of 1925. The all-male college in Oxford, Pennsylvania, had a student body of about 300 students. The university, known as a fine school, had been founded in the mid-19th century by a Presbyterian minister. Its faculty was all white.

Several of Thurgood's classmates became famous. Langston Hughes already was one of the leading poets of the Harlem Renaissance. Kwame Nkrumah would later become president of Ghana.

Thurgood loved college life. He especially enjoyed staying up late with friends, playing cards, and telling funny stories. Sometimes, he would give loud and exciting speeches at pep rallies for Lincoln's football team. Langston Hughes described Thurgood as "the loudest individual in the dormitory—rough, loud, good-natured. . . ." His booming voice became a familiar sound on campus.

Although Thurgood gave the impression that he never studied, he actually worked hard enough to earn good grades. As he left late-night parties, he would tell his friends he was going to bed. Then he would stay up even later, studying for the next day's classes.

To please his mother, Thurgood took some pre-medical courses to prepare for dental school. But he did not do well and decided that dentistry wasn't for him. Instead, he worked hard on other subjects and was chosen to be on the college debating team as a freshman. Two years later, he was one of the top debaters when Lincoln met teams from Harvard University and from several schools in England and Scotland.

A Huge Gap

By the time he was ready to graduate from Lincoln, Thurgood knew what he wanted to do with his life. His debating skills could be put to good use as a lawyer—breaking down the Jim Crow laws that were hurting African Americans.

Thurgood started to think about this in high school when he spent time in the basement memorizing the Constitution. He could see a police station across the street from his school. Too often, he would see black people, without lawyers, taken to the station under arrest. Because they did not know their legal rights, the white officers could scare them into making false confessions.

Thurgood Marshall realized that a huge gap existed between the U.S. Constitution he had been memorizing and many of the laws of the land. The Constitution's words seemed just and proper. Its rules seemed to apply equally to people of all backgrounds. But many laws seemed to defy the Constitution—as did some of the people who enforced them.

Thurgood realized that the Constitution could be used to fight the unfair laws and the harsh treatment they caused. He decided that he could accomplish this goal best by becoming a lawyer.

The campus chapel at Lincoln University.

Thurgood Marshall, second row, second from left, with others in his class at Lincoln University.

The Lincoln University campus.

Catching
the
·Vision·

Chapter 3   1930 - 1933

Key Events in Thurgood Marshall's Life

Thurgood graduates from Lincoln and enrolls at Howard University School of Law in Washington, D.C., where he meets his mentor, Charles Hamilton Houston.

Thurgood excels as a law student and is rewarded with a job in the Howard law library.

Thurgood graduates from Howard University at the top of his class.

Key Events Around the World

The Empire State Building opens in New York City.

Nazi Germany begins persecuting people of Jewish heritage.

1930

1931

1933

1935

1940

1945

1950

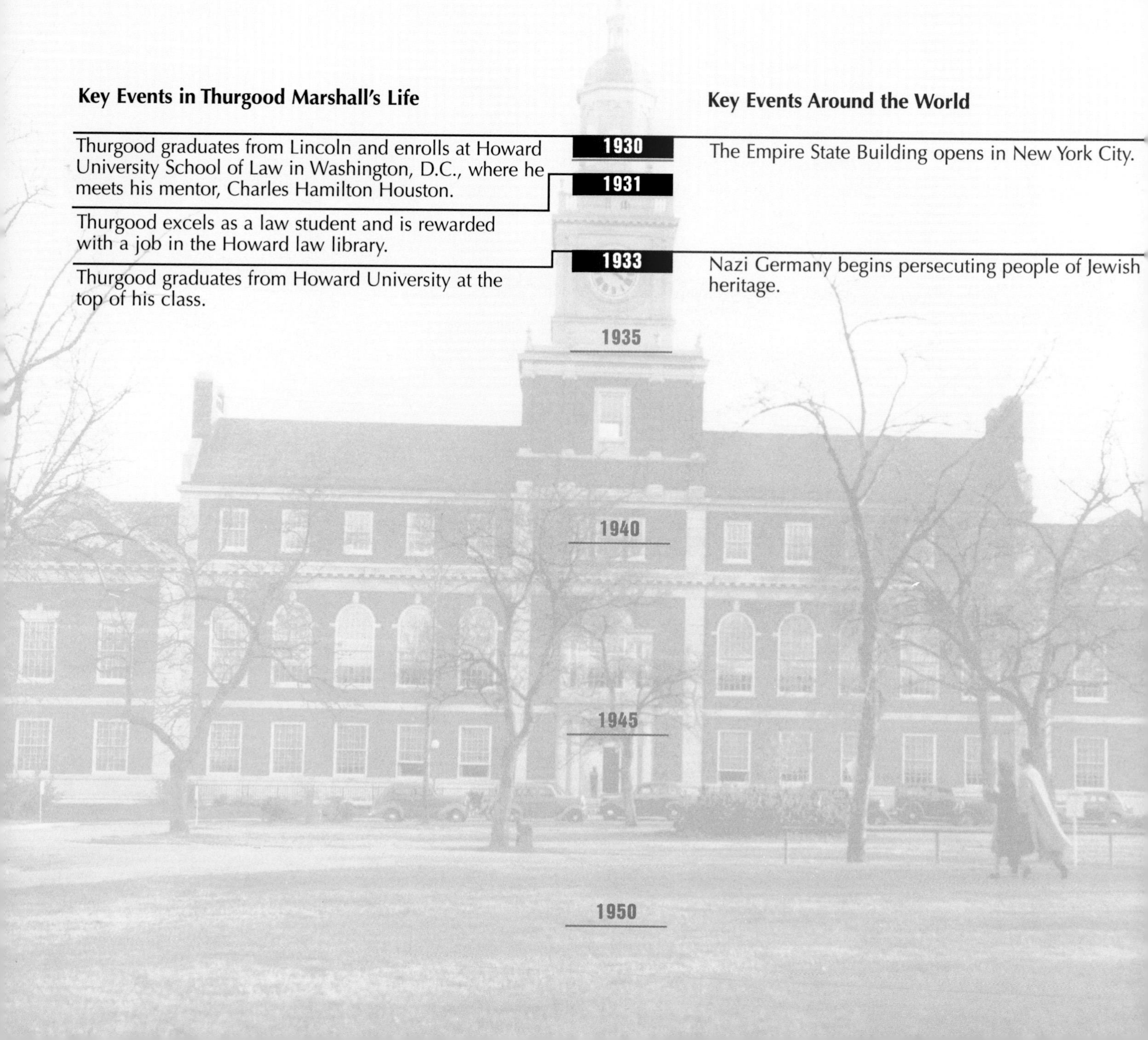

During his years at Lincoln University, Thurgood's change—from a fun-loving, average student into a serious young man—was influenced by several factors. His debating coach, Robert Larabee, gave him strong guidance and helped to push him in this direction. And little by little, Thurgood was beginning to realize how segregation affected his own life.

In his junior year at Lincoln, Thurgood led an effort to keep the school from hiring black professors. He reasoned that black teachers would not be as well qualified as whites. His position angered Langston Hughes, who had led the fight to hire black teachers.

Then, something happened that changed Thurgood's thinking. He and a group of friends went into the town of Oxford to see a western movie. Since the movie theater was segregated, blacks were restricted to the second-floor balcony. But when Thurgood and his friends bought their tickets, they deliberately sat on the main floor, in the "whites only" section. Immediately, someone in the audience yelled, "Why don't you just get out of here and sit where you belong!" But the students ignored the comment, and everyone watched the movie peacefully.

Thurgood's experience at the movie theater caused him to question segregation for the first time. He also changed his mind about his earlier vote against hiring black faculty members at Lincoln. In the fall of his senior year, he led a new debate about the faculty issue—this time arguing in favor of allowing black teachers. The school's all-white hiring policy ended the following year.

The public square in Oxford, Pennsylvania, in the early 1940s.

The entrance to the "colored balcony" at a movie theater.

Vivian Burey Marshall.

A Handsome Couple

Thurgood also was changed by the woman who would become his wife. During his junior year at Lincoln, Thurgood met Vivian Burey, a student at the University of Pennsylvania in Philadelphia. She was a beautiful young woman with dark hair. Thurgood was six feet two inches tall, slender, and handsome. Together, Thurgood and Vivian were an attractive couple. They dated on weekends and quickly fell in love. Originally, they planned to marry after Thurgood graduated, but they couldn't bear being apart. So Thurgood and Vivian married in September 1929, just before Thurgood started his senior year.

Thurgood studied harder than ever before. He also led the debating team to a string of victories. He received his bachelor's degree in June 1930, with his proud wife and parents in the audience. Then he and Vivian returned to Baltimore and moved in with Thurgood's parents, William and Norma Marshall. The young couple would need to live as cheaply as possible for a while, because Thurgood was headed to law school.

University of Maryland School of Law, around 1930.

A Remarkable Mentor

The closest law school was at the University of Maryland in Baltimore. It had a fine law program, and Thurgood could have walked to the campus. But the state's segregation laws kept him from attending. So, in September 1930, he enrolled at Howard University School of Law, in Washington, D.C. At Howard, Thurgood would meet a man who would change his life—Charles Hamilton Houston.

The son of a lawyer, Charles Houston had grown up without experiencing the poverty that affected so many African Americans. He was born in Washington, D.C.—a segregated city but home to one of the richest black communities in America. Attracted by the hope of getting government jobs, many African-American families had moved to Washington after the Civil War. Educated blacks were professors at Howard University. Black doctors saw patients at Freedmen's Hospital. Others ran successful small businesses.

Houston grew up in a city where blacks and whites lived peacefully—but separately. He didn't experience racial hatred until he joined the U.S. Army and served in Europe during World War I. There, he and many other black soldiers were harassed, humiliated, and even threatened—not by the German enemy, but by white American soldiers.

Houston had learned about the law from his father. Sometimes he acted as a lawyer for black soldiers who were accused of misconduct. He lost more cases than he won, however. So Houston made a decision:

> *I made up my mind that I would never get caught again without knowing something about my rights; that if . . . I got through this War, I would study law and use my time fighting for men who could not strike back.*

When he returned home in 1919, Houston enrolled in Harvard Law School—one of the best law schools in America. Harvard had few African Americans at the time, but Houston was an excellent student. He graduated near the top of his class. By the time Houston returned to Washington, he was one of the top young lawyers in the

Charles Houston.

Freedmen's Hospital:
A hospital founded in 1862, on the campus of Howard University, to serve free blacks in the Washington, D.C., area.

Misconduct:
Improper behavior.

The classroom building at Howard University School of Law where Thurgood Marshall attended classes.

The famous lawyer Clarence Darrow (center) meets with Charles Houston (left) and Howard University president Mordecai Johnson (right) at the law school in 1931.

Racial discrimination:

Unfair or unequal treatment and behavior toward a group or an individual because of race.

country. Even so, segregation kept him out of white law firms. Instead, Houston joined the faculty of Howard University School of Law, where he quickly established himself as a top teacher. In 1930, the same year Thurgood entered law school, Houston was appointed dean of the school.

"Iron Pants and Cement Shoes"

Thurgood would never forget his first meeting with Charles Houston. The dean was a tall man with intense brown eyes. He walked into the room where the new class of law students was assembled and said: "Look at the man on your right and look at the man on your left. Next year, two of you won't be here." The students quickly learned that Houston was a demanding teacher who would not tolerate laziness. "He sort of kept your feet to the fire," Thurgood recalled. Houston's attitude earned him the nickname Iron Pants and Cement Shoes.

Houston's stern attitude had a purpose, however. He had a vision. He wanted to train an army of black lawyers to fight against racial discrimination in America. Houston believed that the best place to wage this fight was in the courts. And the best weapon his lawyers would have was the 14th Amendment to the Constitution, which promised equal protection to all American citizens.

An army of black lawyers was needed because there were very few at the time. The state of Alabama had only four black lawyers, for example, even though its black population was nearly one million. Even with enough black lawyers, Houston knew the fight against discrimination would be difficult—even life-threatening. In a 1935 article, "The Need for Negro Lawyers," he described the dangers that these lawyers would face, especially in hostile southern states:

> *If a Negro law school is to make its full contribution to the social system, it must train its students and send them into just such situations. This does not necessarily mean a different course of instruction . . . but it does mean a difference in emphasis.*

Houston understood that he needed to place tough demands on his students because he was preparing them for the most important legal and social battle of the century. This was the "difference in emphasis" that Houston had in mind.

Students in the Howard University School of Law library.

Building an Army

Houston knew that only the most dedicated students could accept his challenge. He wanted black lawyers to become "social engineers"— people working to protect the rights of black citizens. Thurgood was inspired by Houston's words. "This was it," he later said. "This was what I wanted to do as long as I lived." So he studied every minute he possibly could. It wasn't easy, but his efforts paid off. By the end of his first year, Thurgood was first in his class. He was rewarded with a job in the law school library, which helped to pay his tuition. Much more important, Thurgood was brought into closer contact with Houston and other lawyers who were handling civil-rights cases.

A law school class at Howard University in 1939.

Defense attorneys at George Crawford's 1933 murder trial in Leesburg, Virginia.

Verdict:
The decision reached by a jury at the end of a court trial.

Howard University students working in the law school library in 1939.

Houston and the other law professors at Howard were working with the National Association for the Advancement of Colored People (NAACP). It was the nation's leading civil-rights organization. In the early 1930s, the NAACP was developing a legal strategy for challenging segregation laws. The New York-based organization often held meetings in Washington, D.C., at the Howard law library. The school began to help the NAACP with its court cases.

One famous case involved George Crawford, a black man in Virginia who was accused of murdering two white women. Walter White, head of the NAACP, asked Houston to defend Crawford. Thurgood helped Houston with the legal research. They lost the case, but they saved Crawford from the death penalty. The NAACP and Houston treated the verdict as a victory. "If you get a life term for a Negro charged with killing a white person in Virginia, you've won . . . because normally they were hanging them," Thurgood said later.

The *Crawford* case was a turning point in Thurgood's life. It frightened him. It made him realize how powerful the law could be. It could change people's lives—for better or for worse. As Houston had told him, African Americans could not depend on white lawyers to protect them. They needed skilled, dedicated, *black* lawyers. Thurgood was determined to become just such a lawyer. He became Houston's star student, and he worked even harder:

I heard law books were to dig in so I dug deep. I had to commute from Baltimore to Washington [on the train], which meant I got up around five o'clock in the morning and got home around eight o'clock. My first year I lost thirty pounds solely from work—intellectual work, studying. And that's how you get ahead of people.

Another way of getting ahead was to watch the best in action. Sometimes, Thurgood would go across town to watch lawyers argue cases before the U.S. Supreme Court. The most famous lawyer at the time was John W. Davis. A former presidential candidate from South Carolina, Davis presented arguments that made a lasting impression on Thurgood. Whenever he heard Davis in court, he would ask himself whether he ever could be as skilled. "And every time, I had to answer, 'No, never.'"

John W. Davis.

After finishing law school, Thurgood Marshall returned to his
hometown of Baltimore, Maryland, to open his law practice.

JOIN N.A.A.C.P NOW

The

Fight

Begins

Chapter 4

1933 - 1935

Key Events in Thurgood Marshall's Life

Key Events Around the World

1930

Thurgood begins a law practice in Baltimore and volunteers as a lawyer for the NAACP.

1933

1934

Elijah Muhammad becomes the head of the Nation of Islam in Detroit.

Thurgood Marshall and Charles Houston win the *Murray v. Maryland* case.

1935

The Congress of Industrial Organizations (CIO) organizes unskilled workers and promises to end racial discrimination in labor unions.

1940

1945

1950

In 1933, Thurgood Marshall graduated at the top of his class at Howard University School of Law. Just as Charles Houston had predicted, many of the students in Thurgood's freshman class did not finish. Out of Thurgood's original class of 36, only 6 graduated. Houston's methods had been stern, but they produced skilled lawyers, and he made a lasting impression on his students. As Thurgood recalled:

> *I don't know anything I did in the practice of law that wasn't the result of what Charlie Houston banged into my head.*

Thurgood set up his law practice in Baltimore. It was not a good time to begin a career. America was in the midst of the Great Depression—the worst economic crisis in the nation's history. Millions of people were out of work. Back then, there were no unemployment benefits, and thousands of families lost their homes. Many people were on the brink of starvation.

Life was even more difficult in black communities. Jobs, money, and food were scarce. Most of Thurgood's clients could not pay the modest fees he charged for his work. He earned barely enough to support himself and his wife:

> *Once in a while I got a good fee. Then my secretary would immediately take the check to the bank. She'd call her husband and I'd call [my wife], and we'd get the biggest steak in town to celebrate.*

Despite his lack of money, Thurgood held on to his commitment to fight discrimination. He volunteered to handle some of the court cases

Americans hit hard by the Great Depression stand in lines for jobs and food.

Great Depression:
A terrible slump in the U.S. economy, triggered by the crash of the stock market in 1929. Banks closed and millions of workers lost their jobs.

Clients:
People who hire lawyers to defend them in court.

A shoeshine stand in Harlem in the 1930s.

Defendants:

The people against whom a legal action is brought.

Clerk of the court:

A court official who handles the court's records and documents.

for the NAACP. Most of the cases were difficult. Often they involved serious charges against black defendants who faced all-white juries and judges. Thurgood worked hard to become a better lawyer. He knew a loss in court could result in the death penalty for his client. He worked very hard on his arguments and written documents. His special attention to detail was inspired by something a clerk of the court told the law students at Howard:

> *He would say that, with very few exceptions, he could look at [any document] . . . and tell . . . whether it was done by a white or a Negro lawyer. . . . From that day until I stopped practicing law, I never filed a paper in any court with an erasure on it. If I changed a word, it had to be typed all over.*

Thurgood was determined to beat the clerk's test. He did, winning the respect of many white lawyers and judges. During one trial, a white lawyer wanted the judge to check some legal points Thurgood had made. The judge told the lawyer it wasn't necessary. "If Mr. Marshall puts his signature on it, you don't have to check."

Plotting a Strategy

Thurgood's growing success as a lawyer and his constant work for the NAACP led to a new kind of relationship with his former teacher and mentor, Charles Houston. In 1935, two years after Thurgood graduated from Howard law school, Houston became the head of the NAACP's new legal campaign against segregation. That campaign had its roots in a study completed several years earlier. The NAACP had hired a

Thurgood Marshall (center), with Charles Houston and his law partner Edward Lovett, discussing a case in 1934.

Photo courtesy of Baltimore Afro-American Newspapers.

Harvard Law School graduate named Nathan Margold to study the Jim Crow laws.

Margold was a brilliant lawyer who found a possible weakness in the U.S. Supreme Court's 1896 *Plessy* decision. The Supreme Court had insisted on "separate but equal" facilities for both races. Margold pointed out that the Jim Crow laws supported "segregation coupled with discrimination." Most of the facilities provided for blacks in America were separate but *not* equal.

Margold argued that a separate but *unequal* system violated the 14th Amendment. The concept of equal protection under the law was not being followed. Therefore, the NAACP should be able to challenge segregation in court.

Leading the Way

Armed with the report, Walter White, the head of the NAACP, looked for a lawyer to lead the legal fight against segregation. He chose the best lawyer he knew—Charles Houston.

Houston accepted, even though he understood that the NAACP had only $10,000 to pay for the campaign. But he believed that if he could win one or two test cases, it might be enough to encourage more people to join the campaign and contribute more money—even during the Depression. Then, the NAACP could file more lawsuits. It could drown Jim Crow in a flood of legal challenges.

Charles Houston's first segregation target was education. First, he would try to force a southern state to provide equal schools for black

Fourteenth Amendment

The 14th Amendment to the Constitution guarantees equal protection under the law. All Americans, regardless of race, are entitled to equal rights. Even though it was ratified in 1868, the Supreme Court did not uphold it to end segregation until 1954.

Document courtesy of National Archives.

Charles Houston seated at his desk.

A teacher conducts school classes in a church in Gee's Bend, Alabama, in 1937.

children. Then, he would try something that would hit segregation supporters where it really hurt—in their wallets. Houston would demand equal pay for black teachers.

Houston would plan the NAACP effort, but the actual court cases would be handled by some of those talented black lawyers he had trained at Howard. They were the "social engineers" who shared his vision. And Thurgood Marshall was at the top of his list.

Strange Fruit

The first thing Houston asked his former student to do was to go with him on trips through the South. Houston wanted to see for himself how schools for white children differed from those for blacks. He recorded many of the schools on film, using a small movie camera.

Houston and Marshall were shocked by what they saw. Many of the "colored" schools in southern states had dirt floors and lacked electricity or water. Holes in the roof let the rain in, soaking the children. None of the schools for white children had such poor conditions.

During their travels together, Thurgood and his former teacher became close friends. They talked about how different—and how much better—America would be once segregation ended.

One day, Thurgood was sitting in Houston's car by the side of a road, eating an orange. He and Houston always carried fruit with them when they traveled. They wanted to have something to eat if they could not find a restaurant that served black customers.

A black child approached Thurgood and stared at the orange he was eating. So Thurgood grabbed another orange and handed it to the boy:

The kid did not even take the peeling off. He had never seen an orange before. He just bit right through it and enjoyed it.

Thurgood understood what that simple action meant. Something as ordinary as an orange was strange to a child in a segregated school. He promised himself that he would do whatever he could to end this unfair system.

Taking the Plunge

Thurgood's first step in the battle to end segregation began in November 1934. He learned that the University of Maryland School of Law had turned down yet another African American. He was Donald Gaines Murray, a recent graduate of Amherst College, in Massachusetts. State officials told Murray to apply instead to Princess Anne Academy, a college for black students. But Princess Anne had no law school.

Thurgood believed that Murray could be an ideal plaintiff in a lawsuit against the university. Murray was bright, well spoken, handsome, and well educated. Thurgood believed this could be one of Charles Houston's test cases. He also had a personal reason for taking the case—Murray was a distant relative, and he had attended Lincoln University for two years.

Thurgood asked Charles Houston to help him, and in January 1935, they filed a lawsuit in Baltimore. The trial began the following June.

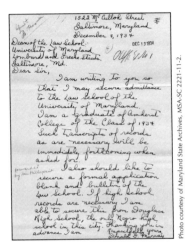

Donald G. Murray's letter requesting admission to the University of Maryland School of Law in 1934.

Plaintiff:
The person who files a lawsuit.

Thurgood Marshall (left) and Charles Houston (right) work with Donald Murray on their 1935 lawsuit against the University of Maryland.

Princess Anne Academy, Maryland.

Guaranteed:
Assured that a particular condition or outcome will occur.

University of Maryland, College Park, in the 1930s.

On the first day, the courtroom was packed with curious onlookers. Word of the trial had spread quickly through the city's black community. Thurgood's wife and parents were there to cheer him on.

This was Thurgood's biggest challenge so far. He was nervous and excited. Drawing on his experience, Houston was calm and confident— a commanding presence in the courtroom. He began by pointing out that Murray had satisfied all of the admissions requirements for the University of Maryland School of Law. It was clear that Murray's application had been denied because of his race. This action violated Murray's right to equal protection under the law, as guaranteed by the 14th Amendment.

The University of Maryland's lawyer, Charles T. LeVinnes, replied that the segregation law required the school to turn away black students. He also said that the state had satisfied its responsibility to Murray, and to other black students, by establishing Princess Anne Academy. LeVinnes added that Maryland provided scholarships for black students who wanted to attend out-of-state law schools instead. The scholarships were $200 per year.

Challenging the System

In a gruff voice, Judge Eugene O'Dunne asked LeVinnes how a $200 scholarship could cover the costs of attending an out-of-state university. He also asked whether the state would agree that Murray satisfied all requirements for admission. LeVinnes had no answer for the first question. For the second question, he admitted that Murray was qualified.

Houston and Marshall's first witness was Donald Murray. He testified that he had lived in Maryland all of his life. He wanted to attend law school but had not been allowed to enroll at the university. Murray, a forceful speaker, made a strong impression on Judge O'Dunne.

The next witness was Raymond A. Pearson, the president of the University of Maryland. He seemed uncomfortable the whole time he testified. Houston got him to agree that Murray's application satisfied the school's admissions requirements. Pearson also admitted that Maryland did not have enough money to cover scholarships for every black student who wanted to go to an out-of-state school.

As the trial continued, Houston and Marshall presented a powerful case. They convinced the judge that Princess Anne Academy was *not* equal to the University of Maryland. The academy's facilities were less well equipped. Its school year was one month shorter than the University of Maryland's. Its teachers were less qualified—and they earned less than white teachers. The two lawyers also proved that black students faced another obstacle. They had to go to law schools *outside* of Maryland, but in order to practice law in the state, students would have to pass an exam on state laws. The only law schools that focused on state law were *inside* the state of Maryland!

A Stunning Outcome

Both men shared the closing argument in the trial. Thurgood was no longer nervous. He spoke with confidence. His deep, loud voice filled the courtroom. He argued that the state of Maryland had a constitutional duty to educate students of all races equally—whether or not they

Testified:
Declared under oath in a court of law.

A letter from University of Maryland president Raymond A. Pearson to Donald G. Murray denying his admission to the law school in 1934.

Top: Dr. Raymond A. Pearson, president, University of Maryland at College Park, 1926-1935.

Thurgood Marshall walks with Donald Murray in 1935, the year of their case against the University of Maryland.

attended separate schools. But Maryland was not fulfilling its duty. It excluded African Americans from its law school without creating a "separate but equal" law school for them.

Judge O'Dunne ruled so quickly that he surprised everyone. The University of Maryland would have to provide an equal education for *both* black and white students. He ordered the university to admit Donald Murray to its law school in the fall of 1935.

The university's lawyers were stunned, as the spectators cheered wildly in the crowded courtroom. They applauded Charles Houston and Thurgood Marshall as they walked out. The two men had won the first successful challenge of a Jim Crow law. Thurgood was especially proud of this victory, because segregation once had kept him from attending law school in his own state. He found his wife, Vivian, in the crowd and danced joyously with her. As he later told a reporter, "It was sweet revenge, and I enjoyed it to no end."

Front page of *The Afro-American* for the week of June 22, 1935, reporting the results of the *Murray* case.

Victories
and
Dangers

Chapter 5   1935 - 1946

	Key Events in Thurgood Marshall's Life		Key Events Around the World

Key Events in Thurgood Marshall's Life

Key Events Around the World

1935

1936

Thurgood Marshall and Charles Houston get the U.S. Supreme Court to order the University of Missouri to admit Lloyd Gaines.

1937

Jesse Owens wins four gold medals in the Berlin Olympics.

Joe Louis becomes the heavyweight boxing champion of the world. Amelia Earhart's plane disappears.

1939

Thurgood wins equal pay for black teachers in the entire state of Maryland.

1940

Opera singer Marian Anderson performs at the Lincoln Memorial, after being denied the use of Constitution Hall by the Daughters of the American Revolution.

Thurgood has murder convictions overturned for four black men in Florida.

1941

Thurgood wins a case for black passengers against the Illinois Railroad.

Thurgood wins voting rights for blacks in Texas primary elections.

1944

1945

Germany and Japan surrender, ending World War II. The United Nations is established.

Thurgood has a segregation law overturned for interstate bus passengers and escapes an angry mob in Columbia, Tennessee.

1946

1950

1955

The *Murray* decision sent a message of hope to the black community. Ever since *Plessy v. Ferguson*, African Americans had no choice but to obey the segregation laws and endure the frequent insults of white people. But *Murray* gave a badly needed boost to the civil-rights movement. As Charles Houston had predicted, black lawyers began to challenge segregation laws in other states.

The next big case for Charles Houston and Thurgood Marshall took place in Missouri. Lloyd Gaines was a 1935 graduate of Missouri's Lincoln University. He applied to the University of Missouri School of Law, which turned him down because of his race. Gaines sued, and Charles Houston and two other lawyers from St. Louis represented him.

The Gaines case was similar to *Murray*. Lincoln University had no law school, so Missouri provided out-of-state scholarships for black students. During the trial, the state's lawyers agreed that Gaines qualified for admission and that he was turned down only because of his race. Even so, the judge ruled against Gaines.

A Legal Weapon

Houston appealed the verdict to the Missouri Supreme Court. He argued that the Missouri court should follow the Maryland court's ruling in the *Murray* case. Lloyd Gaines should be admitted to the University of Missouri School of Law. But the court ruled that Missouri had done enough by establishing Lincoln University as an excellent institution for black students. The state had no further responsibility.

Civil-rights movement:
An organized effort that fought for equal rights for all citizens, regardless of race, gender, or ethnic group.

Lloyd Gaines at his trial against the University of Missouri in 1936.

Tate Hall, which houses the law school of the University of Missouri in Columbia.

Brief:

A lawyer's written summary that explains his or her case to a judge.

Precedent:

A court decision in one case that helps judges decide future cases with similar facts.

The 1936 Supreme Court.

Houston appealed again, this time to the U.S. Supreme Court. Thurgood wrote the brief for the case. The university's lawyers argued that Gaines did not need to be admitted to Missouri's law school. They explained that he *should* have applied to law school at Lincoln University, *which then would have been required to establish a separate law school for him!*

The Supreme Court rejected this strange argument. The judges ordered Missouri to admit Gaines to the university's law school. Once again, Houston, Marshall, and the NAACP had won. They had convinced the Supreme Court that it would be impossible for Missouri to establish a separate law school for black students that was equal to the state's law school for white students.

From now on, lawyers who argued similar cases could use a powerful new legal weapon. A Supreme Court victory meant that the *Gaines* decision could be used as a precedent.

These two court victories—*Murray* and *Gaines*—were important first steps in the NAACP's campaign against segregation. But the two court victories had helped only a small group of African Americans—students who wanted to attend graduate schools. Now Houston and Marshall needed to find an issue that would benefit many more people. They decided to try to win equal pay for black teachers.

Money Troubles

In most school systems, black teachers were paid only half as much as white teachers. Houston and Thurgood were certain that a successful suit against unequal teacher's pay would shake segregation to its core. The NAACP also would benefit. Grateful teachers were more likely to join the NAACP, and their membership dues would help fund more lawsuits against segregation.

Although Thurgood felt happy and proud about the courtroom victories, he worried about his family. By the middle of 1936, Thurgood's mother, Norma, still worked as a teacher in Baltimore's black schools. His father, William, could not find work during the Depression. Norma had to support them both. To add to their troubles, Thurgood's brother, Aubrey, had developed tuberculosis. The good hospitals in Baltimore were for "whites only," so Thurgood got him admitted to Bellevue Hospital in New York. There, Aubrey had one of his diseased lungs removed. Norma had to pay for Aubrey's care with the small salary of a "colored" teacher.

Thurgood had money troubles of his own. He was in debt because most of his Baltimore clients could not afford to pay him. Desperate, he wrote a letter to Houston, complaining that "something must be done about money!"

Houston's reply set Thurgood on a road into history. He invited the 28-year-old powerhouse to join the NAACP as a full-time staff lawyer. Thurgood was thrilled! He wrote to Walter White, head of the NAACP, "I have an opportunity now to do what I have always dreamed of doing!"

Norma Marshall, Thurgood Marshall's mother, with her first-grade class.

An NAACP poster urging people to join and "Finish the Fight!"

Tuberculosis:

A highly contagious disease that infects body tissues, especially those of the lungs and throat, causing fever, weight loss, and coughing.

Apartments in Harlem in New York City.

A Dream Come True

Thurgood and Vivian moved to New York City. They found an apartment on Edgecombe Avenue, in Harlem's Sugar Hill section. There, Thurgood settled in with a new group of friends, doing what he liked best. By day, he fought civil-rights battles. At night, he partied, played cards, and swapped tall tales with his buddies. His new job didn't solve his money troubles, however:

> *After a couple of years, the board of directors had a great big meeting, and raised my salary . . . they raised me from $2400 to $2600. And when I got home . . . I told [Vivian] about it [and] she said, "Oh, that's fine." Then after a half hour or so, she said, "By the way, how much is that a week?"*

Thurgood's answer: about four dollars. To earn extra money, he delivered groceries—just as he had as a child!

A Preacher's Passion

Despite his constant lack of money, Thurgood threw himself into his work. He often traveled to his home state of Maryland to explain the NAACP's strategy for fighting segregation. He spoke to African-American community groups in dozens of cities and towns. He explained how the NAACP planned to use the courts to fight for equal pay for black teachers. Thurgood always had been a forceful speaker, but

A portrait of Thurgood Marshall in 1936.

now he inspired audiences with the passion of a preacher. And teachers began to volunteer as plaintiffs in test cases.

Thurgood filed the NAACP's first equal-pay case in Montgomery County, Maryland, in December 1936. He represented William Gibbs, the principal of the county's school for black students. Before the case went to trial, the lawyer for the county's school board contacted Thurgood. The lawyer suggested a settlement. By July 1937, Montgomery County agreed to raise the salaries of black teachers to the level of white teachers over a two-year period.

A year later, Charles Houston decided to leave his job as the NAACP's chief counsel in the antisegregation campaign. Thurgood was promoted to the position. At the age of 30, just seven years out of law school, he became the top lawyer for the most powerful civil-rights organization in the United States. Despite his promotion, Thurgood continued to rely on Charles Houston's advice.

Armed with a victory in the *Gibbs* case, Thurgood filed more lawsuits in Maryland's counties. He planned to sue every school system in the state, if necessary, until all black teachers earned equal pay. There was a drawback to this strategy, however. It took too much time! Thurgood needed a court ruling that would apply to the whole state. That's what happened in December 1939. He won a judgment for black teachers in *Mills v. Board of Education of Anne Arundel County.* As a result of this decision, Maryland passed a law requiring equal salaries for black and white teachers—the first such law in the nation.

Thurgood Marshall (second row, far right) with the national board of directors of the NAACP, in Detroit, Michigan, around 1937.

Settlement:
An agreement between the plaintiff and the defendant in a lawsuit that has been reached without a court trial.

Counsel:
A lawyer or group of lawyers hired to represent an organization or company.

Judgment:
The official decision in a court trial.

Roy Wilkins (left), Walter White (center), and Thurgood Marshall (right) stand in front of NAACP headquarters.

Legislature:

The body of individuals that writes the laws for a state or country.

Unanimously:

With all individuals in agreement.

Primary election:

An election held by political parties to determine their candidates in an upcoming general election.

High-Court Victories

Over the next several years, Thurgood argued so many civil-rights cases that he became a familiar figure in the U.S. Supreme Court. He won 29 of his 32 cases, many of which are still important precedents.

In 1940, for example, Thurgood defended four black men who had been convicted of murdering a white merchant. The men were jailed for five days without being allowed to talk to a lawyer. They were beaten several times, until they confessed to the crime. In the case, *Chambers v. Florida,* Thurgood argued that the men had confessed only because they had been beaten. This brutal treatment violated their constitutional rights. The Supreme Court agreed and overturned the convictions.

In 1941, Thurgood won an important transportation case. In *Mitchell v. United States,* he challenged a segregation law that affected train passengers. Mitchell was a black member of the Illinois state legislature. He was forced to leave his first-class seat and move to a car without running water or toilets. After hearing Thurgood's arguments, the Supreme Court voted unanimously that the railroad's facilities for black passengers were not equal to those for whites.

In a 1944 case, *Smith v. Allwright,* Thurgood fought a Texas law that prevented African Americans from voting in primary elections. Since the Democratic Party dominated the state at the time, the candidate who won the primary election was certain to win the general election. The Supreme Court voted eight to one to outlaw this practice.

In 1946, a black woman named Irene Morgan was arrested for refusing to move to the back of a Greyhound bus traveling from Virginia to Baltimore. A Virginia state law required black passengers to sit in the rear of buses. Morgan's lawyer sued the state, claiming the law was unconstitutional. Thurgood handled the appeal. He convinced the Supreme Court that because Morgan was an interstate passenger, the state law didn't apply.

Thurgood's impressive string of court victories made him well known in legal circles. He earned a reputation as a skilled lawyer who never was rude or threatening. He always was polite to judges and other lawyers—even when they insulted him. Once he even helped an opposing lawyer find the legal citation for a case he was arguing.

Thurgood was polite, but he also was strong-willed. The spirited child had grown up to be a forceful man. He often was described as friendly and funny, but he never backed down in an argument—and he knew the law. More than anything, Thurgood was determined to be as respected as any white person. In court, he fought anyone who tried to keep black people from seeking better lives.

A Brush with Death

Thurgood's actions began to attract the attention of white bigots. Traveling through the South, arguing case after case, Thurgood and other NAACP lawyers sometimes faced threats and danger—just as Charles Houston had warned.

NAACP attorneys and defendants in the 1946 Columbia, Tennessee, trial of 25 black men accused of murder.

Interstate:
Involving or connecting two or more states.

Citation:
A reference to written laws and rulings or to statements by other people.

Bigots:
People who strongly dislike anyone of a different race or religious belief.

Police in Columbia, Tennessee, search a group of black men arrested during rioting.

Headlines from the Baltimore *Afro-American* cover three cases Thurgood Marshall argued before the Supreme Court.

Thurgood had a personal brush with death in 1946. He was in Columbia, Tennessee, where he had just won a case for 25 black defendants charged with murder. After the victory, Thurgood and two other NAACP lawyers were stopped by a police car as they were driving out of town. A group of angry police officers spilled out. They charged Thurgood with drunk driving and ordered him into their car. They warned the other lawyers to drive away.

Thurgood's worried friends followed the police car as it swerved onto a side road toward a river. There, they could see a mob of angry white men waiting for the car. But when the police realized they had been followed, they turned their car around and took Thurgood back to town. They brought him before a local judge:

> He told me to blow my breath in his face. I rocked him I blew so hard, because I hadn't had a drink in two days. He [told the officers,] "That man is not drunk and he hasn't even had a drink." So he told me I was free to go.

Thurgood was released, but the police were determined to stop him again. He made his escape by switching cars. Just as he had feared, the driver of the decoy car was stopped by the police. The driver was beaten badly.

After that experience, people who heard Thurgood make speeches or argue a case noticed a difference in him. His voice wasn't as loud, and he didn't tell as many funny stories. The terror of that night stayed with him for a long time.

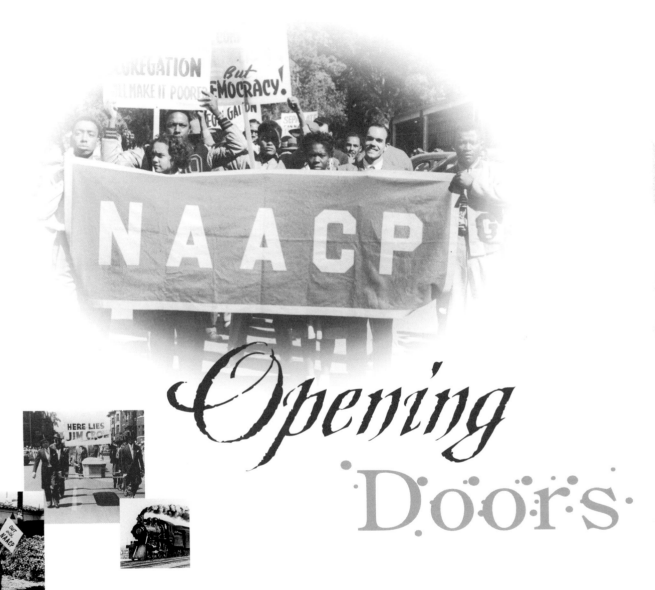

Opening Doors

Chapter 6

1946 - 1948

Key Events in Thurgood Marshall's Life

Key Events Around the World

1945

1946

Thurgood persuades the Supreme Court to outlaw segregation on all buses traveling between states.

President Truman appoints a Civil Rights Committee

1947

The NAACP asks the United Nations (UN) to investigate racial inequities.

William Marshall, Thurgood's father, dies at age 65.

1948

Howard University School of Law helps Thurgood practice his arguments for the Supreme Court by hosting mock trials.

Eleanor Roosevelt leads the way to a UN Declaration of Human Rights.

1950

1955

1960

1965

By the mid-1940s, Thurgood Marshall had an impressive list of court victories. Top lawyers and judges—white and black—respected Thurgood. He got along well with just about everyone. Even some of the bigoted judges and sheriffs were friendly to him. Everybody enjoyed his jokes and stories, but they also respected his understanding of the law. When Thurgood Marshall took aim at a legal issue, people knew that something important was about to happen.

The next target for Thurgood and the NAACP was housing discrimination. Black families moving from the rural South to cities in the North often had a difficult time finding decent places to live. They frequently ran into covenants that kept them out of white communities.

Originally, covenants were written to keep homes from being turned into factories or stores. Racial, or "restrictive," covenants, however, were used to prevent white homeowners from selling their property to black buyers. In many American communities, restrictive covenants also were used to keep out Jewish families.

An "Invisible Wall"

Thurgood knew all about restrictive covenants. The first city to adopt them had been Baltimore, Maryland—his hometown! He also knew that covenants would be difficult to challenge because they were private contracts. In 1926, the U.S. Supreme Court had ruled that the 14th Amendment did not apply to actions between individual citizens. The Court's ruling encouraged more restrictive covenants. By the late 1920s, *every* American city with a black population had them.

Thurgood Marshall as an attorney for the NAACP in the 1940s.

Covenants:

Written promises or agreements between two or more people.

Children play on the lawn of their suburban neighborhood in Yonkers, New York, in 1942.

Ghettos:

Areas of cities where groups of minority people are forced to live due to legal, economic, or social pressures.

Children play in the yard of a housing project in Chicago, Illinois, in 1942.

People in a Miami, Florida, neighborhood protest against new black neighbors.

Restrictive covenants separated the races. They created ghettos. Charles Houston said the covenants trapped black families inside an "invisible wall." And Thurgood believed that restrictive covenants, by keeping blacks and whites apart, made it easier for the two groups to resent each other.

Restrictive covenants also were unfair. They allowed ghetto property owners to charge black families high prices for poor housing. Because the covenants confined black families only to certain neighborhoods, owners had more people competing for a limited amount of housing. The result was higher prices. The situation got worse after World War II, when black soldiers qualified for government housing loans. They had more money to spend, but covenants kept them out of decent neighborhoods. So property owners could charge even more.

In spite of these obstacles, some black families managed to buy better homes. One way was to find a "straw man"—a white person who pretended to be the homebuyer. Under this arrangement, the straw man bought the property, then immediately resold it to a black buyer—at a profit. Another way was to find a white homeowner who would ignore the covenants. Either way, black homebuyers had to pay higher prices, allowing home sellers to make bigger profits.

Fighting Covenants

Thurgood Marshall and the NAACP began filing dozens of lawsuits to challenge racial covenants. They used the same strategy they had used to fight segregated colleges and unequal pay for black teachers. They tried to turn one of the lawsuits into a test case before the U.S. Supreme Court.

The case that met their need was *Shelley v. Kraemer*. The Shelley family lived in St. Louis, Missouri. They had moved there from Mississippi in 1939. At the time, the Shelleys were renting a house in one of the few neighborhoods available to black families. The house, located in an area near the Mississippi River, was nearly falling apart. Even so, the Shelleys had to pay a high rent.

After a few years, the Shelleys had saved enough money to make a down payment on a home. They chose a house on Labadie Avenue, in a white neighborhood. The minister at their church found a straw man, who bought the house, raised the price, and sold it to the minister. The minister then sold the house to the Shelleys for $5,700—nearly double its original price. The Shelleys were happy to own a nicer home than the one they had been renting. They moved into it in October 1945.

Almost at once, the Shelleys received an eviction order. One of their new white neighbors, the Kraemer family, had filed a lawsuit claiming that a covenant kept the Shelleys from buying the house. Other white neighbors helped to pay for the lawsuit.

A group of black real-estate agents came to the Shelleys' defense. They hired George Vaughn, an African-American lawyer from St. Louis, to represent the family. Vaughn and the Shelleys won the case in the local court. The Kraemers appealed, and the decision was reversed by the Missouri Supreme Court.

Backed by the NAACP, Vaughn then took the case to the U.S. Supreme Court. The Shelleys' case would be heard with three other cases involving covenants, and the four cases were given one name: The *Restrictive Covenants Cases*. Thurgood Marshall handled one of the cases

Down payment:

Part of the purchase price of something, paid at the time of purchase. The rest of the money is due later.

Eviction:

Forceful removal from a property, such as a house or apartment.

Residents in Atlanta, Georgia, gather to protest a new black family in the neighborhood.

A mock courtroom at the law school of Howard University.

Colleagues:
Co-workers—people who work in the same office or at the same job.

from Detroit, Michigan, and Charles Houston managed two others from Washington, D.C.

As soon as the Supreme Court began hearing the cases in January 1948, three of the nine justices had to excuse themselves from the trial—they owned property governed by racial covenants!

As the NAACP's chief lawyer, Thurgood took extra care to prepare. He returned to Howard University School of Law to participate in several "mock" trials. These practice sessions allowed Thurgood to try out his arguments with colleagues before presenting them in court. Six Howard law professors acted as Supreme Court justices, raising questions that the justices might ask during the upcoming trial. Thurgood also invited Howard University law students to sit in the mock courtroom and he encouraged them to ask questions.

Not a Private Matter

The mock trials proved to be highly useful to Thurgood. One law student earned groans from the group when he asked a long, rambling question. But that same question was asked by a Supreme Court justice during the real trial in May 1948!

Thurgood argued that racial covenants were not strictly private matters. Restrictive covenants had a broader impact, he told the justices, because state and local governments enforced them. But Thurgood didn't stop there:

This case is not a matter of enforcing an isolated private agreement. It is a test as to whether we have a united nation or a country divided into areas and ghettos solely along racial and religious lines.

Despite Thurgood's solid preparation and strong legal argument, he worried that the Supreme Court justices would refuse to support him. They asked him tough questions about people's rights to sell their property freely—including the right not to sell to someone. Thurgood feared that he would be defeated. He also worried that George Vaughn would be too emotional:

We all worried about this guy. So we tried to tell him what to argue and he would not listen. He wanted to argue the Thirteenth Amendment [which outlawed slavery].

Photo courtesy of National Archives, 67-1984.

Thurgood Marshall often retyped his own documents if they contained errors.

Knocking on the Door

But Vaughn's passionate argument stunned everyone in the courtroom. The son of a former slave, Vaughn stood before the justices and called racial covenants the biggest weakness of American democracy. In a booming voice that echoed through the building, he declared: "The Negro knocks at America's door and cries, 'Let me come in and sit by the fire. I helped build this house.'" Vaughn drove home his point by rapping his knuckles loudly on the lawyers' table.

Newspaper courtesy of Library of Congress and Baltimore Afro-American Newspapers.

Newspaper headlines announce the NAACP's victory in the restrictive covenants cases on May 8, 1948.

Men in white tie and tails bear a coffin and a sign to demonstrate against Jim Crow segregation laws in 1944.

Solicitor general:

The second highest U.S. government lawyer. Only the attorney general ranks higher.

Unconstitutional:

Not permitted by the U.S. Constitution.

A whistling Thurgood Marshall leaves an NAACP convention in Atlantic City, New Jersey.

It was a dramatic moment, and it eased Thurgood's worries about the case. Then Philip Perlman, the solicitor general of the United States, also spoke out against restrictive covenants:

> *Attempts are made by such devices as restrictive covenants to hold [African Americans] in bondage, to segregate them, to hem them in so that they cannot escape from the evil conditions under which so many of them are compelled to live.*

Perlman had been asked to support the NAACP's case by none other than President Harry S Truman. But Perlman also had a personal reason for speaking. His Jewish family had been victims of Baltimore's restrictive covenants. For more than an hour, Perlman supported the arguments of Thurgood's team. In the end, the Supreme Court agreed. On the grounds that covenants violated the 14th Amendment, the justices declared that restrictive covenants were unconstitutional.

The Court's ruling made headlines across America. The decision was cheered as a major turning point in the battle against segregation. And Thurgood Marshall became a well-known name. Some people even honored him with a new nickname: Jim Crow Buster.

No More Separate Tables

Tables

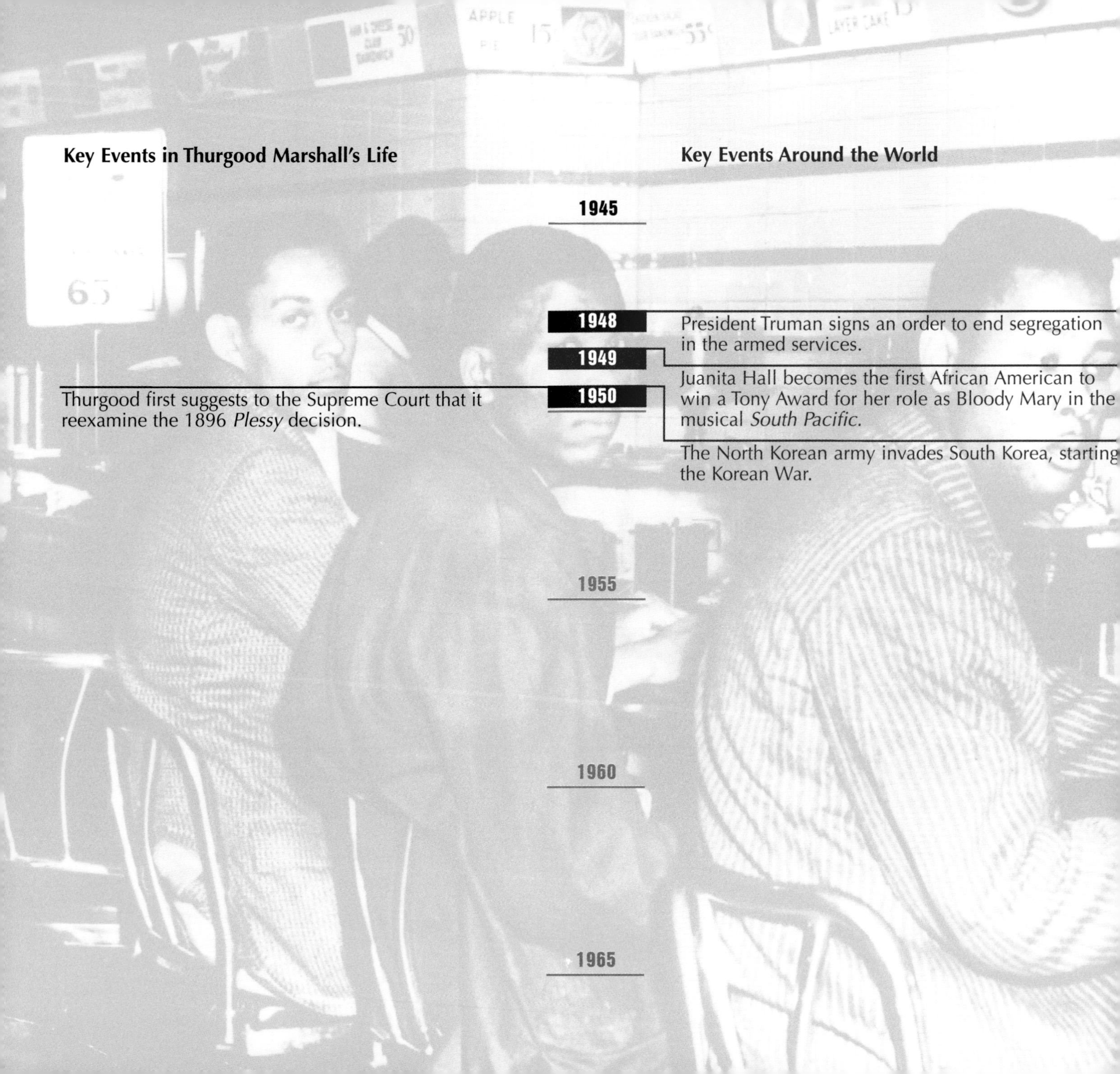

Key Events in Thurgood Marshall's Life

Key Events Around the World

1945	

Thurgood first suggests to the Supreme Court that it reexamine the 1896 *Plessy* decision.

1948 President Truman signs an order to end segregation in the armed services.

1949 Juanita Hall becomes the first African American to win a Tony Award for her role as Bloody Mary in the musical *South Pacific*.

1950 The North Korean army invades South Korea, starting the Korean War.

1955

1960

1965

$\mathcal{B}$y the late 1940s, hundreds of thousands of students were enrolling in colleges and universities, more than at any time in American history. Returning World War II veterans were eligible under the GI Bill to borrow money from the government to pay for their educations. Many took advantage of this opportunity, creating a new generation of college graduates. Thousands of black veterans sought college degrees, but most faced discrimination.

Thurgood Marshall, Charles Houston, and other NAACP lawyers saw the changing situation in education as an opportunity to end segregation in the schools. Up until now, the NAACP had been following the plan recommended by the Margold report in the 1930s. In case after case, they had forced school systems to provide equal resources to black students and teachers. In a few cases, black students had been admitted to formerly all-white schools.

But the pace of this progress had been slow. Now, the rising number of black college applicants called for action on a larger scale. "We shifted to hitting [segregation] straight on," Thurgood recalled. He and the other lawyers grew more determined than ever to defeat the Jim Crow laws:

> *While it was true that a lot of us might die without ever seeing the goal realized, we were going to have to change directions if our children weren't going to die [under segregation] too.*

GI Bill:

A law passed by Congress after World War II that gave money to veterans for college and job training, and low-cost loans to buy houses and start businesses.

Veterans:

People who have served in the armed forces.

An all-black flying unit of the U.S. Army Air Corps during World War II.

Photo courtesy of National Archives and CORBIS/Bettmann, NA001196.

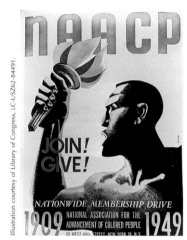

NAACP poster featuring 1936 Olympic champion runner Jesse Owens.

Dismissed:

A lawsuit that has been rejected by a court, usually for lack of evidence.

Evidence:

Information given at a trial to support a lawyer's argument.

"Why Should She?"

The NAACP decided to flood the courts with lawsuits challenging segregation in colleges and universities. Its lawyers would base their arguments on the U.S. Supreme Court's *Gaines* decision. In that case, the Court had ordered Missouri to admit Lloyd Gaines to its all-white law school because the state had no law school for black students. This new effort would introduce a new word to the American public—integration.

Over the next several years, Thurgood argued three important school integration cases before the Supreme Court. The first involved Ada L. Sipuel, who had graduated with honors from the State College for Negroes in Langston, Oklahoma. Sipuel applied for admission to the University of Oklahoma's law school, but she was rejected. The university was segregated, but the state did not provide a separate graduate school for black students.

Sipuel's lawyer, Roscoe Dunjee, was head of the NAACP's Oklahoma branch and was the editor of the *Oklahoma Black Dispatch* newspaper. His lawsuit against the university did not go well at first. The trial court dismissed the case, and the Oklahoma Supreme Court rejected Dunjee's appeal. The justices ruled that Sipuel should have asked the state to establish a law school for black students. Since she didn't ask, the justices decided that Sipuel had no right to ask for admission to the university.

In January 1948, Thurgood appealed the Oklahoma court's decision to the U.S. Supreme Court. But the Sipuel case made him uneasy because it had been dismissed. Thurgood preferred cases that had gone to trial, because the trial records included evidence about unequal school facilities. That evidence would strengthen his presentation. Even so, he argued the case.

The Supreme Court justices seemed to be sympathetic. When a lawyer for the state of Oklahoma claimed that Sipuel wasn't "willing to recognize the state's segregation policy," Justice Robert Jackson snapped, "Why should she?" Four days later, the Court issued its decision. In a short opinion, the justices wrote that Sipuel's application to the university had been denied solely because of her race. "[Sipuel] is entitled to . . . a legal education," the Court ruled. "The State must provide it for her [according to] the equal protection clause of the Fourteenth Amendment. . . ."

Thurgood Marshall and Ada Sipuel, the first African American to enroll at the University of Oklahoma.

Back to Oklahoma

The University of Oklahoma did not give up. It roped off an area of the state capitol building in Oklahoma City and called it the "Langston Law School." Three black educators were hired as faculty members.

Thurgood was outraged. He telephoned Ada Sipuel and told her, "Forget it . . . don't even show up in the same block of that law school!" Thurgood returned to the Supreme Court and demanded that the state of Oklahoma be forced to obey the Court's order. To his surprise and disappointment, the Court rejected his motion. Since the state had established a "law school," the justices ruled, the Court's original order had been obeyed. If Thurgood wanted to challenge the state's action further, he would have to go back to the Oklahoma courts and start over.

Motion:
A formal request to a judge.

Demonstrators in Norman, Oklahoma, protest Ada Sipuel's lawsuit against the University of Oklahoma.

Fraud:

A trick used to cheat someone.

Thurgood accepted the challenge. He also brought some of the finest lawyers in the country with him—the deans of the law schools at Harvard, Yale, Columbia, and the University of Pennsylvania. These experts traveled to Oklahoma for free to support the case. They were willing to help Thurgood because of his reputation as a fine lawyer!

Using his impressive witnesses and his own strong arguments, Thurgood tried to convince the Oklahoma court that the Langston Law School was a fraud. Its only purpose, he declared, was to prevent the integration of the University of Oklahoma law school. In private, even the judge hearing the trial would admit that Ada Sipuel was treated unfairly. He told Thurgood later that the case had opened his eyes to the harm of segregation. Even so, the judge ruled against the NAACP and Sipuel.

Kept Apart

Thurgood was working on another case in Oklahoma at about the same time. This one involved George W. McLaurin, a 68-year-old teacher who had been hired as one of the three professors at Langston University. McLaurin had applied to the School of Education at the University of Oklahoma. The school accepted McLaurin, but when he began to attend classes, he found that he was separated from the white students.

The university seated McLaurin in a small area in the back of the main classroom that had been a broom closet. He was given a separate desk in the library, away from the main reading room. He could not eat in the cafeteria at the same time as the white students. Everywhere

McLaurin went, the school put up signs reading "Colored," to show the elderly professor where he could sit. The only bright spot for McLaurin was the sympathy he received from some of the white students—who tore down the signs as soon as they appeared.

When the case went before the U.S. Supreme Court, university officials scrambled to change the arrangements. They gave McLaurin a seat in the classroom, but they put him in a row marked "Colored." He was allowed to eat in the cafeteria at the same time as the white students, but he had to sit at a separate table.

A Small Victory

While Thurgood was managing the Sipuel and McLaurin cases, he also filed a suit for Heman Marion Sweatt, a letter carrier who had applied to the University of Texas School of Law in Austin. As in the other cases, the university agreed that Sweatt was qualified to attend but it turned him down because he was black.

The state court reached an unusual decision. Instead of forcing the university to admit Sweatt to its law school, the court gave Texas officials six months to create a new law school for black students. The university rented a few rooms in Houston, Texas, and hired two black lawyers as faculty. The new "law school" became a branch of Prairie View University, an all-black college that had been created several years earlier.

Heman Marion Sweatt appears in court in Austin, Texas, in 1947.

Black students protest the "separate but equal" rule in Texas schools.

Testimony:
Information given by a person who has sworn to tell the truth.

Six months passed, and the court reviewed the progress of the university. The judge ruled that the small, pathetic Houston school was "substantially equal" to the all-white law school in Austin.

Thurgood appealed the judge's ruling. The university quickly took steps to improve the facilities. The black law school was moved to Austin, where three rooms were set aside in a building across from the state capitol. Black students were allowed to use the large law library in the capitol building, and faculty members from the University of Texas came to teach them. The state government approved three million dollars to build better facilities at Prairie View. It set aside one hundred thousand dollars of that money to build a law school.

Once again, Thurgood brought in legal experts. They testified that the black law school was inferior to the one at the University of Texas. The segregationist judge, Roy Archer, remained unconvinced. But Thurgood managed to enjoy one small victory in the case. A group of white law students from the university attended the trial. They were impressed by Thurgood's arguments—and by Sweatt's passionate testimony that he "never" would go to a segregated university. When the dean testified that segregation was needed to protect white students, the white law students booed him!

Questioning "*Plessy*"

The *Sweatt* and *McLaurin* cases reached the U.S. Supreme Court at the same time, in April 1950. By now, Thurgood Marshall was a familiar face in the courtroom. He continued to be nervous before a Supreme Court appearance. But as soon as he began his argument, he became calm, relaxed, and in command. As he walked around the courtroom, gesturing with his glasses, his loud voice echoed in the large court chamber.

This time, Thurgood was more nervous than usual. He also spoke more quietly, because his arguments in both cases contained a hint of something larger. He suggested that the Court should take another look at *Plessy v. Ferguson,* the case that had established the "separate but equal" policy.

George McLaurin sits in a separate area outside a classroom at the University of Oklahoma.

Photo courtesy of Howard University.

The Power of a Picture

Thurgood's efforts in the *McLaurin* case received some unexpected help from the press. A photograph of George McLaurin appeared in national newspapers and magazines, showing him at his separate desk, in a far corner of a classroom at the University of Oklahoma. He was leaning forward, straining to hear the instructor. It was a powerful image of how insulting segregation could be.

The old saying that "one picture is worth a thousand words" proved to be true. McLaurin's photograph may have influenced the Supreme Court justices nearly as much as Thurgood's arguments. The justices were not ready to grant Thurgood's request to reconsider the

Headlines in the Baltimore *Afro-American* predict the Heman Sweatt case may bring the death of Jim Crow laws.

Photo courtesy of Library of Congress and Baltimore Afro-American Newspapers.

Plessy decision, but their two short opinions in the *Sweatt* and *McLaurin* cases hinted that the "separate but equal" ruling had flaws.

In the *Sweatt* case, the Court agreed that the facilities of the new Texas law school for black students were not equal to those for white students:

> *The University of Texas Law School possesses qualities which . . . make for greatness in a law school. . . . It is difficult to believe that one who had a free choice between [the black and white] law schools would consider the question close.*

The Court reached a similar conclusion in the *McLaurin* case, even though the situation was somewhat different. The Court had decided that segregation *within* a university also violated the 14th Amendment:

> *[The university] handicapped [McLaurin]. . . . Such restrictions impair and inhibit his ability to study, to engage in discussions and exchange views with other students and, in general, to learn his profession.*

Meanwhile, the *Sipuel* case was settled out of court. The University of Oklahoma decided to admit Ada Sipuel and several other black students. At first, the law school seated them in the back of the classroom in a row marked "Colored." But after a few months, the signs came down. Sipuel and the other black students could sit where they wanted.

Photo courtesy of Library of Congress, LC-USZ62-117796.

George McLaurin shakes hands with fellow students at the University of Oklahoma.

Armed for Battle

Armed with the *Sweatt* and *McLaurin* decisions, Thurgood Marshall knew that the NAACP could challenge segregation directly. He was convinced that he finally had enough evidence to prove that segregation would always allow states to give more support and resources to white schools than to black schools.

The Supreme Court's ruling in *McLaurin* had gone even further. The justices had understood that there was more to education than bricks and mortar. Students learned from one another by talking and exchanging ideas. This could not happen in a system where black and white students were separated. By seating George McLaurin in a "colored" section of the classroom and forcing him to sit at a separate table in the library or cafeteria, the state of Oklahoma had cut him off from interacting with his fellow students.

The Court had begun to question the whole system of segregation. These two decisions had prepared the way for Thurgood to challenge it. As Charles Houston had written in 1947:

> *The NAACP is making a direct, open, all-out fight against*
> *segregation. . . . There is no such thing as "separate but equal."*
> *Segregation itself [means] inequality.*

Thurgood hoped to focus the Supreme Court's attention on segregation's human cost. Once the Court understood that segregation resulted in second-class citizenship, it might agree that the equal-treatment requirements of the 14th Amendment were being denied:

Charles Houston in court.

Thurgood Marshall discusses the NAACP's legal action against school segregation with a parent in 1949.

Neither Congress nor anyone else can say that you get equality of education in a segregated school. The Fourteenth Amendment requires equality. The only way to get equality is for two people to get the same thing, at the same place, and at the same time.

Thurgood's next move was to look for cases that could bring this issue to the attention of the entire nation.

Attacking Segregation

Chapter 8

1950 - 1952

Key Events in Thurgood Marshall's Life

Child psychologist Kenneth Clark is hired by the NAACP to study how school segregation has affected black children.

Thurgood visits South Korea and Japan to investigate charges of racism in the armed services.

Thurgood is threatened with death if he ever returns to Clarendon County, South Carolina, where he has filed a school desegregation case.

Key Events Around the World

Senator Joseph McCarthy accuses the U.S. State Department of hiring Communists.

Mary Church Terrell, born in 1863, leads the court fight to desegregate restaurants in Washington, D.C.

National political conventions are broadcast on nationwide television for the first time.

1950

1951

1952

1955

1960

1965

1970

$\mathcal{F}$or as long as Thurgood Marshall fought the Jim Crow laws in court, he was under pressure from Charles Houston, his mentor and former teacher. Houston constantly scolded him for not defeating segregation fast enough. Although the two men were close friends, they were very different. After working hard on his court presentations, Thurgood liked to enjoy himself. He went out with Vivian or with his friends almost every night. Houston, on the other hand, worked around the clock. He hardly ever took time off to relax.

By the late 1940s, this lifestyle had begun to affect Houston's health. The long hours without sleep or exercise had weakened his heart. Even so, he was determined not to rest until he defeated segregation. He often said, "I'd rather die on my feet than live on my knees."

In a sense, that's exactly what happened. In April 1950, at the age of 54, Charles Houston died of a sudden heart attack. He was rushed to Freedmen's Hospital, near his beloved Howard University law school, but the doctors could not save him.

Houston's death threw Thurgood into a deep depression. At first he did not think he could go on without his friend's guidance. But soon he realized that he had to finish the fight Houston had begun 15 years earlier. He could not let his mentor down. After attending Houston's funeral in Washington, Thurgood returned to New York, determined to carry on.

Charles Houston as a law professor at Howard University.

A Plan of Attack

Thurgood Marshall and the NAACP decided that the only sure way to end segregation was to have the U.S. Supreme Court strike down a Jim Crow law. If one Jim Crow law was declared to be unconstitutional, sooner or later they all would fall.

This bold tactic meant Thurgood would need to attack the 1896 *Plessy v. Ferguson* decision. He could not simply suggest that the Court review *Plessy,* as he had done in the *Sweatt* and *McLaurin* cases. Instead, he would have to demand that the Court reverse *Plessy*—once and for all.

Thurgood knew that such a task would be the biggest challenge of his life. It would be a much tougher fight than forcing state universities to admit a few qualified black students. Desegregating public schools—to allow white and black children to sit together in classrooms across the country—would take everything he had learned about the law and about being a lawyer. Thurgood needed to be more skillful than any other lawyer who might oppose him before the Supreme Court.

Collecting Lawsuits

Thurgood could not simply ask the Supreme Court to declare that segregation was unconstitutional. The Court would have to issue that ruling as part of its decision in a case. And Thurgood could not file just one lawsuit. To win a decision this large, he would have to pull together several strong cases from different states.

The task took more than two years and involved six cases. The first, *Briggs v. Elliot,* was filed in Clarendon County, South Carolina, in May

Reverse:
Change the outcome of a lower court ruling or send the case back to the lower court for a second ruling.

Desegregating:
Ending racial segregation, or separation, by allowing equal access to facilities and services for all citizens.

1950. A group of black parents, led by a navy war veteran named Harry Briggs Jr., had demanded that Clarendon County spend an equal amount of money on *all* of its schoolchildren. The school system had been spending an average of $179 per year on each white student, but only $43 per year on each black student. Thurgood took the case because he had won several other cases in South Carolina. He had developed good working relationships with some of the state's important judges.

Jimmy Byrnes, the governor of South Carolina at the time, knew all about Thurgood Marshall. He realized that with Thurgood involved in the *Briggs* case, Clarendon County might lose in the Supreme Court. He asked the state legislature for money to begin building better schools for black children. Although the lawmakers agreed to the governor's request, they warned him that they would close every school in the state if the Supreme Court ordered desegregation.

Byrnes did not want a crisis over the schools. To boost Clarendon County's chances of winning in court, he turned to a close friend for help—John W. Davis, the same lawyer Thurgood had admired as a law student at Howard University. Davis agreed to advise the South Carolina legal team.

The second case was filed three months later, when a group of black parents tried to integrate Sousa Junior High School in Washington, D.C. They argued that the local high school for black students was run down and overcrowded. James Nabrit Jr. and George E. C. Hayes represented the parents. Nabrit, a law professor at Howard University, took the case as a favor to Charles Houston. Later, Thurgood assigned Hayes to help on behalf of the NAACP.

Recess at a country school for black children near Lake Village, Arkansas.

A run-down elementary school for black children in South Boston, Virginia, in the 1930s.

Strike:

A temporary stopping of work or other activities to protest a problem or condition.

NAACP attorneys Spottswood Robinson and Oliver Hill with students from Prince Edward County, Virginia.

Top: Spottswood Bolling, one of 12 black children seeking admittance to an all-white high school in Washington, D.C., in 1950, and his mother.

In April 1952, black students in Prince Edward County, Virginia, went on strike to protest the poor condition of their high school. They swore to remain on strike until the school board agreed to build a new school. The students wrote a letter to the NAACP asking for help. In reply, Thurgood sent two Richmond lawyers who were friends of his. The lawyers, Oliver Hill and Spottswood Robinson, were so impressed by the students' determination that they agreed to represent them in court. Thurgood had his third case.

The fourth case was filed in Claymont, Delaware, a suburb just a few miles north of Wilmington. Claymont's school for white children was a new and well-equipped building. Black students had to take a bus to Howard High School in Wilmington, an old building surrounded by factories and warehouses.

The fifth case was filed by Sarah Bulah, a white woman who had adopted a black child. When her child reached school age, Bulah was forced to drive past the well-built elementary school for white children in her Wilmington neighborhood. She had to take her child to the shabby, one-room schoolhouse for black children.

Thurgood assigned both Delaware cases to Jack Greenberg, a graduate of Columbia University Law School in New York City. Greenberg was the one white member of the NAACP team.

Linda Brown's Trip to School

The sixth and most famous of the school desegregation cases started in Topeka, Kansas. Seven-year-old Linda Brown lived near a nice new elementary school. But because she was black, she had to leave home at 7:40 each morning and cross railroad tracks to reach her bus stop. There, she waited for the bus that would take her across town to the school for black children.

Linda's father, Oliver Brown, was angry about his daughter's long trip to school each day. On February 14, 1951, he and Robert Carter—a young NAACP lawyer assigned by Thurgood Marshall to represent the Brown family—filed what would become one of the best-known court cases in American history: *Brown v. Board of Education of Topeka*.

Thurgood believed the *Brown* case might turn out to be the most important of the six. Topeka's schools were unusual. For the most part, its schools for black and white children *were* equal. Thurgood wanted to show that black children were harmed by being kept apart from white children. Dealing with this issue might force the courts to look beyond the "separate but equal" issue of the *Plessy* decision. The courts might have to decide whether school segregation was unconstitutional.

One by one, the six cases worked their way through the lower courts. And one by one, the judges ruled against the NAACP. But two of the rulings had language that might become helpful when the cases reached the Supreme Court. In *Brown*, the Kansas court made an important statement about the effect of segregation:

Linda Brown in 1953.

Segregation of white and colored children in public schools has a [harmful] effect upon the colored children . . . [and] the policy of separating the races . . . usually . . . [implies] the inferiority of the Negro group.

Likewise, in a ruling that covered both Delaware cases, the state court found that segregation results in black children's "receiving educational opportunities which are substantially inferior to those available to white children."

Despite these conclusions, the Kansas and Delaware courts refused to overturn school segregation. The *Plessy* decision, the judges wrote, kept them from doing so. If *Plessy* was to be reversed, the Supreme Court would have to do it.

Photo courtesy of Library of Congress, LC-USZ62-115760.

Overturn:

Reject or reverse a decision.

Child psychologist Kenneth Clark and his wife, Mamie Phipps Clark.

Psychology:

The study of the human mind and behavior.

"The Doll That Looks Bad"

The lower court losses did not bother Thurgood Marshall. He had expected them. He knew that the real battle over school desegregation was yet to come. It would take place in the Supreme Court. What mattered now was collecting enough evidence against segregation. Part of that evidence would have to come from expert witnesses—highly respected people who would testify that segregation was harmful, whether or not facilities for blacks and whites were equal.

One of the experts Thurgood hired was Kenneth Clark, a pioneer in child psychology. Clark was an African-American professor at the City College of New York. He and his wife, Mamie, had developed a series of tests that showed how segregation affected black children age three to seven.

In one of the tests, the Clarks used four dolls. Two of them were brown and two were white. The Clarks first asked the children to identify the race of the dolls. Then they gave the children a series of directions:

1. Give me the doll you like to play with.
2. Give me the doll that is the nice doll.
3. Give me the doll that looks bad.
4. Give me the doll that is a nice color.

When the children chose the doll that was nice or the doll they liked best, most black children from segregated schools picked the white doll. When they chose the doll that looked bad, most of them picked the brown doll.

The Clarks also used a coloring test. They gave black children a set of crayons and some pictures to color—a leaf, an apple, an orange, and a mouse. If the children colored those objects correctly, the Clarks gave the children drawings of people. They asked the children to pretend that they were the people in the pictures and to color them correctly. Most of the black children colored the people white or an unrealistic color, such as yellow, red, or green. The Clarks believed that the children were rejecting their own color because of the effects of racism. Several studies by other experts agreed with their findings.

When Thurgood asked Kenneth Clark to repeat his experiments in Clarendon County, Clark came up with the same results. Segregation had affected the way the county's black children thought of themselves.

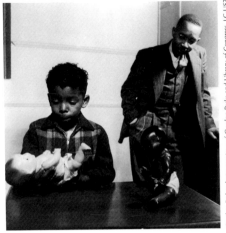

Kenneth Clark conducts the "doll test" with a young boy in 1947.

Even with Clark's findings, Thurgood lost the South Carolina case in the lower court, as he had expected to do. This meant that all six school desegregation cases were headed to the U.S. Supreme Court. The outcome would affect the lives of all American schoolchildren—and their parents—for a long time.

Escape from an angry mob, Columbia, TN

Brown, Chambers, Gaines, Mitchell, Smith, Restrictive Covenants, and other Supreme Court cases, Washington, D.C.

Murray case, Baltimore, MD

Gibbs case, Montgomery County, MD

Crawford case, Richmond, VA

Briggs case, Clarendon County, SC

Sipuel and *McLaurin* Cases, Oklahoma City, OK

Central High School desegregation case, Little Rock, AR

Sweatt case, Austin, TX

Smith case, Houston, TX

Bus boycott, Montgomery, AL

Thurgood Marshall's Travels

For nearly 25 years—from 1933 to 1957—Thurgood Marshall traveled to many parts of America in his campaign to end Jim Crow segregation laws.
This map shows the locations of some of Thurgood's most important legal cases.

The
Showdown

Chapter 9

1952 - 1955

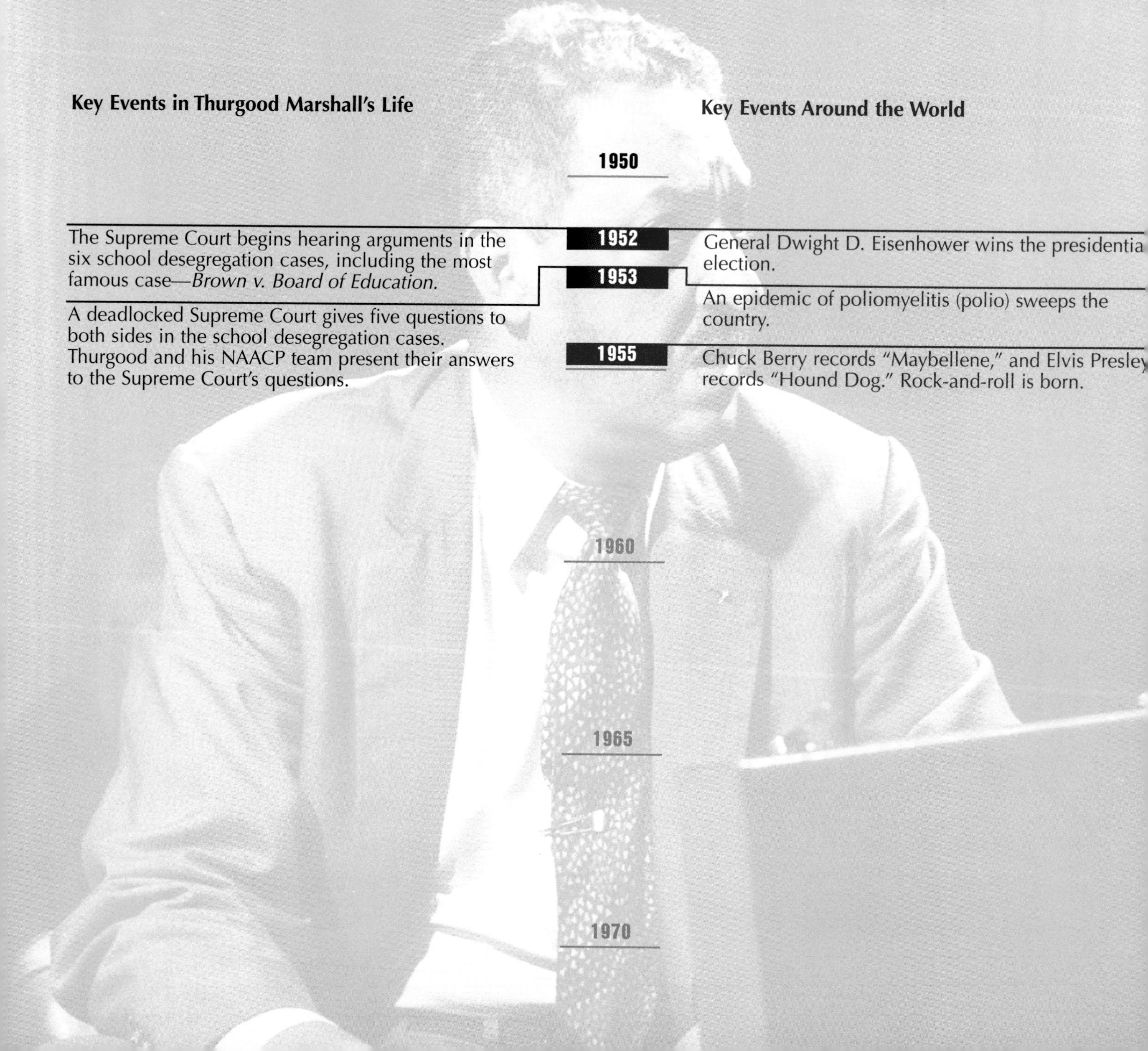

Key Events in Thurgood Marshall's Life

Key Events Around the World

1950

1952

The Supreme Court begins hearing arguments in the six school desegregation cases, including the most famous case—*Brown v. Board of Education.*

General Dwight D. Eisenhower wins the presidentia election.

1953

A deadlocked Supreme Court gives five questions to both sides in the school desegregation cases. Thurgood and his NAACP team present their answers to the Supreme Court's questions.

An epidemic of poliomyelitis (polio) sweeps the country.

1955

Chuck Berry records "Maybellene," and Elvis Presley records "Hound Dog." Rock-and-roll is born.

1960

1965

1970

$\mathcal{E}$arly in the morning of December 9, 1952, a line of people stood outside the Supreme Court Building in Washington, D.C. It stretched down the building's white marble steps and snaked its way toward the U.S. Capitol. By the time guards opened the doors at 9:30 a.m., more than 200 people were waiting in the cold. Many had stood there overnight. They were waiting for a chance to attend the "trial of the century"—six cases, pulled together as *Brown v. Board of Education*. At last, segregation was going on trial!

Thurgood Marshall had been preparing his legal arguments for nearly two years. His work schedule had been as tough as Charles Houston's. As a result, his own health had begun to suffer. No longer the tall, lanky kid from Baltimore with movie star good looks, Thurgood now was a gray-haired, overweight man with dark circles under his eyes. He looked old for his 44 years of age.

Thurgood's emotional health was not good, either. In public, he still was the jovial, wisecracking person that everyone liked. In private, however, he struggled with fear and self-doubt. Sometimes he felt as though he carried the burden of all African Americans on his shoulders. In a sense, he did.

If Thurgood lost the school desegregation cases in the Supreme Court and the *Plessy* decision remained in place, the mistake could set the civil-rights movement back a long time. A second chance to end Jim Crow might not come along for many years. Thurgood remembered a grim warning from Charles Houston: "Doctors can bury their mistakes. We don't have that luxury."

Spectators line up outside the Supreme Court to hear arguments for *Brown v. Board of Education* in 1954.

Thurgood Marshall on the steps of the Supreme Court.

Thurgood faced increasing criticism from African Americans, who worried that he might indeed lose the Supreme Court case. A few black newspapers claimed that he was not fighting hard enough to end segregation. They thought the Kenneth Clark experiments would distract the high court from the issue of segregation. Other black lawyers complained that Thurgood was drawing too much attention to himself.

Climbing the Marble Stairs

Ignoring the doubt, Thurgood and the six other NAACP lawyers briskly climbed the marble stairs of the Supreme Court to begin their arguments. Robert Carter opened the session with the NAACP's argument in the Linda Brown case. Thurgood followed, presenting his argument in the South Carolina case. As usual, Thurgood started to relax as he argued his case.

Less experienced lawyers might find the nine black-robed justices intimidating. But after 14 years and dozens of cases before the high court, Thurgood actually felt comfortable. In a confident voice, he explained that his case would prove that school segregation violated the constitutional rights of black children. It injured the "development of the personalities of children," he said, "destroying their self-respect."

John W. Davis represented South Carolina. Now age 79 and retired, he looked every bit as impressive as he was when Thurgood came to watch him as a law student. Calm and gracious, Davis approached the justices. He addressed them with the confidence of a man who had faced them 139 times before.

Davis stressed that South Carolina was working to make its school facilities equal. Not only that, but the Supreme Court's *Plessy* decision gave South Carolina the right to classify students on the basis of race. Davis challenged the NAACP's claim that segregation violated the 14th Amendment. "There is no reason," Davis said, "why this Court should reverse the findings of 90 years."

Thurgood Marshall then stood up and made a brief rebuttal. He reminded the justices that nothing in the U.S. Constitution supported laws that discriminated against persons because of their race.

When Thurgood and his fellow NAACP lawyers had presented their arguments in all six cases, they left the building. There was no need to wait. The justices would have to discuss the cases among themselves, a process that could take months. But not even the sharpest legal experts could have predicted what happened next.

Rebuttal:
A legal response that tries to defeat the opposing side's arguments.

A Deadlocked Court

After more than six months of debate, the Supreme Court justices failed to issue a verdict. To everyone's surprise, they sent a series of questions to the lawyers on both sides. What did Congress intend when it enacted the 14th Amendment? Was an end to school segregation one of its goals? How would school integration be managed? The NAACP team and the opposing lawyers would have to answer these questions by October 1953, when the high court would meet again.

Thurgood and his team spent the summer doing intense research, seeking the advice of experts, and debating among themselves. They

John W. Davis and Thurgood Marshall during *Brown v. Board of Education.*

Reconstruction:

The period after the Civil War, from 1867 to about 1879, when the federal government started a plan to restore southern states to the Union.

Supremacy:

Superiority or dominance.

decided to argue that the 14th Amendment was intended to prevent segregation. They would focus on the nation's legal history during the Reconstruction period after the Civil War. Finally, they would try to show that the 1896 *Plessy* decision was flawed. Instead of promoting equality, *Plessy* promoted segregation to preserve white supremacy.

In September 1953, the Supreme Court's chief justice, Frederick Vinson, died suddenly. President Dwight D. Eisenhower appointed a stunning replacement—Earl Warren, the governor of California. The president's choice gave Thurgood reason to hope. He knew that Vinson had opposed the NAACP's position and that Warren would be more sympathetic. If Warren voted against segregation, as Thurgood expected, the NAACP almost certainly would win.

"Racial Prestige"

On December 7, 1953, Thurgood Marshall began three days of new arguments. Almost one full year had passed since his first presentation. Drawn by the promise of an exciting courtroom drama, spectators filled the Supreme Court Building again.

The NAACP had done its homework. Spottswood Robinson presented historical evidence showing that the Supreme Court usually protected individual rights over the rights of states. Then Thurgood rose to begin his argument. He pointed out that the 14th Amendment gave federal courts the right to outlaw segregation. But the nine justices seemed unmoved.

Thurgood Marshall confers with NAACP lawyers Harold Boulware (left) and Spottswood Robinson (right) in December 1953.

Opposing lawyer John Davis then argued that the people who signed the 14th Amendment never intended to end segregated schools. He noted that the Freedmen's Bureau had set up separate schools throughout the South during Reconstruction. Davis further claimed that segregation was now so firmly established in America that the Court could not end it. South Carolina, Davis said, was asking the Court to preserve its right to enforce segregation. The high court, he said, could not end segregation "on some fancied notion of racial prestige."

Thurgood was furious at Davis for his remarks, but he focused his emotions for his finest performance. When Thurgood rose to present his rebuttal, one newspaper reported that "all of the Supreme Court justices came to attention." He agreed that the cases were about "racial prestige":

> *Exactly correct. Ever since the Emancipation Proclamation, the Negro has been trying to get the same status as anybody else, regardless of race.*

What his clients wanted, Thurgood explained, was whatever "prestige" they would gain from a recognition of their rights as American citizens. He reminded the justices that equality was at the heart of these cases. Then, Thurgood issued a daring challenge:

> *The only way that this Court can decide this case [against us] is to find that, for some reason, Negroes are inferior to all other human beings.*

Thurgood's voice was filled with emotion and confidence. The entire courtroom was silent as he finished his statement and sat down.

Freedmen's Bureau:
A government organization started in 1865 to help formerly enslaved people receive education, housing, and supplies.

Racial prestige:
Social standing based on race.

Photo courtesy of CORBIS/Bettmann, BE085983.

Thurgood Marshall sits below a portrait of Supreme Court justice Louis Brandeis, a longtime supporter of civil rights and the Howard University School of Law.

Supreme Court chief justice Earl Warren.

Inherently:
Naturally, or essentially.

Adjourned:
Stopped, either temporarily or permanently.

A victorious Thurgood Marshall with NAACP lawyers George E. C. Hayes (left) and James Nabrit Jr. (right) on May 17, 1954.

Stunning News

The wait for the high court decision seemed to take even longer than before. Finally, on May 17, 1954, Chief Justice Earl Warren read the Court's decision. The Court could not agree on the intent of the 14th Amendment, Warren admitted, but one thing was clear:

> *Segregation of children in public schools solely on the basis of race . . . deprives the children of the minority group of equal educational opportunities. To separate [black] children from others of similar age and qualifications generates a feeling of inferiority . . . that may affect their hearts and minds in ways unlikely ever to be undone.*

Justice Warren ended the Court's ruling with words that Thurgood Marshall had spent a lifetime waiting to hear: "Separate educational facilities are inherently unequal." These words were followed by even more stunning news. The high court's decision was unanimous—all nine justices had voted to end segregation.

As the Court adjourned, the crowd rushed outside. Spectators on the steps of the building cheered wildly. Newspaper reporters rushed to telephones to call in their stories. The next day, banner headlines around the world announced the Supreme Court's decision. African Americans were overcome with joy.

At the NAACP headquarters in New York, the cheers and congratulations turned into a party that lasted almost all night. Thurgood Marshall had become a national celebrity. Reporters hounded him for interviews. Telegrams and letters poured into his office.

Newspapers across the country displayed his photograph, opposite a portrait of the nine Supreme Court justices. His phone rang nonstop. One of the first calls was from John Davis, who congratulated Thurgood on his victory. "I beat him," Thurgood said later, "but you can't name many people who did."

The *Brown* decision, as it quickly became known, seemed to exhaust Thurgood. As he said later, "I was so happy, I was numb." His only regret was that Charles Houston had not lived long enough to see his legal strategy pay off. "The school case was really Charlie's victory," Thurgood told a newspaper reporter. He added:

> *I think that, even in the most prejudiced communities, the majority of people have some respect for truth and some sense of justice, no matter how deeply hidden it is at times.*

Thurgood knew Houston would have shared his dream that the *Brown* decision would help America to live up to the promise of its Constitution.

Sitting on the steps of the Supreme Court, a mother explains the Supreme Court's *Brown* decision to her daughter.

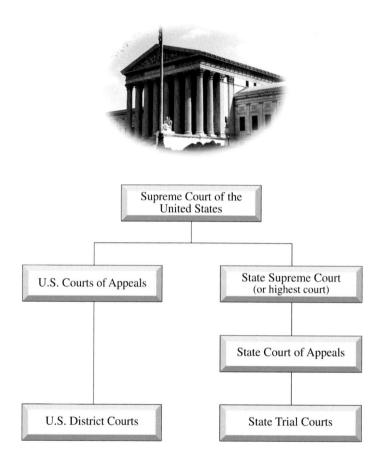

U.S. Court System

The court system in the United States consists of local, state, and federal courts,
each with different areas of responsibility. The U.S. Supreme Court is the highest court in the land.
Its nine justices can change the decision of any other court, including the state supreme courts.

The
Judge's
Chair

Chapter 16

1955 - 1967

Key Events in Thurgood Marshall's Life

Key Events Around the World

	1955 — The American Federation of Labor (AFL) merges with the Congress of Industrial Organizations (CIO).
In February, Vivian Burey Marshall, Thurgood's wife of 25 years, dies of cancer. In December, Thurgood marries Cecilia "Cissy" Suyat.	**1956** — The NAACP defends Rosa Parks and Martin Luther King Jr., leaders of the bus boycott in Montgomery, Alabama.
Thurgood's first son, Thurgood Marshall Jr., is born.	**1957** — Congress passes the Civil Rights Act of 1957 and sets the Civil Rights Division of the Department of Justice.
The NAACP, led by Thurgood Marshall, represents nine black students trying to integrate Central High School in Little Rock, Arkansas.	**1958** — Public schools in Prince Edward County, Virginia, are closed to avoid having to obey a court order to integra
	1959
Thurgood's second son, John William Marshall, is born.	**1960** — Berry Gordy starts the Motown Record Company in Detroit, Michigan.
Thurgood's mother, Norma, dies at age 74. Thurgood is appointed to the United States Court of Appeals for the Second Circuit.	**1961** — Democrat John F. Kennedy wins the presidential election, the youngest person ever to hold the office.
	1963 — The Communist government of East Germany begins building the Berlin Wall to keep its citizens from escaping to the West.
	1964
President Lyndon B. Johnson appoints Thurgood solicitor general of the United States. The Marshalls move from New York City to Washington, D.C.	**1965** — A massive March on Washington focuses attention on the civil-rights movement. Martin Luther King Jr. delivers his "I Have a Dream" speech. President Kennedy is assassinated in Dallas, Texas.
President Johnson nominates Marshall to the Supreme Court of the United States on June 13.	**1967** — President Johnson signs the Civil Rights Act of 1964, banning discrimination in public places. Martin Luther King Jr. receives the Nobel Peace Prize.
	College students across the country demonstrate against U.S. participation in the Vietnam War.
	Race riots break out in many American cities.
	1970
	1975

A few months after the *Brown* decision, tragedy struck Thurgood's life again. His wife, Vivian, finally told him something she had been keeping from him for some time—she was dying of cancer. Thurgood immediately took time off to stay home and take care of her. "She would have done the same thing for me," he said later. Vivian Marshall died on February 11, 1955, on her 45th birthday. She and Thurgood had been married for 25 years.

Thurgood was tired and full of sadness—yet he still had work to do. Segregation was not going to disappear just because the U.S. Supreme Court had ruled it was unconstitutional. Integration would take a long time. Thurgood had realized this almost as soon as the *Brown* decision was announced. He told the NAACP lawyers: "I don't want any of you to fool yourselves. It's just begun, the fight has just begun."

"All Deliberate Speed"

Whenever the Supreme Court decides that a person's rights are being violated, it usually orders the violation to be stopped immediately. But Thurgood Marshall knew that the Court's action following the *Brown* case would be different. White parents all over America were outraged at the thought of their children going to school with black children. Although Thurgood understood the anger of white parents, he believed that their children could make the change. As he had said during his Supreme Court argument:

"...With All Deliberate Speed"

Illustration courtesy of Baltimore Afro-American Newspapers.

A political cartoon portrays Thurgood Marshall as an engineer on the NAACP's Desegregation Special.

Thurgood Marshall and Delaware NAACP lawyer Louis Redding (left) confer at the Supreme Court in 1955.

I know in the South, where I spend most of my time, you will see white and colored kids going down the road together to school. They separate and go to different schools and they come out and they play together. I do not see why there would necessarily be any trouble if they want to go to school together.

Thurgood and the NAACP were willing to allow school systems time to desegregate. But they wanted the Supreme Court to set a deadline. Thurgood asked the Court to require integration by the beginning of the 1956 school year. But on May 31, 1955, the Supreme Court rejected the NAACP's request. Instead, the Court sent all six segregation cases back to their states with the same order—begin integrating "with all deliberate speed."

The ruling bothered Thurgood. If the states had no deadline for desegregation, they would try to stretch the process out as long as possible. Also, school desegregation was only one part of the problem. Even though Thurgood and the NAACP had won the backing of the U.S. Supreme Court, they still faced an uphill battle to end other types of segregation in America, especially in the South.

The Bus Boycott

In December 1955, Rosa Parks, a small, soft-spoken woman, was arrested in Montgomery, Alabama. She had been sitting on a bus, riding home from her job as a tailor's assistant. Tired from a long day of working, she had refused to move when the bus driver ordered her to give up her seat to a white passenger.

In response to the arrest of Rosa Parks, Montgomery's African-American community organized a bus boycott. During the next several months, blacks refused to ride the city's buses and found other forms of transportation. In many cases, they simply walked. As time passed, the nearly empty buses began to lose money.

The leader of the boycott was a 26-year-old Baptist minister named Martin Luther King Jr. He had left his home in Atlanta, Georgia, 18 months earlier to serve as pastor of Montgomery's Dexter Avenue Baptist Church. King not only led the boycott, he spoke out against the city's segregation ordinances. He preached at his church and spoke at rallies on the streets of Montgomery.

The events in Montgomery became the subject of headlines across the nation. Millions of Americans also watched news reports about the boycott on television, and they saw and heard King speak out against segregation. As a result, Montgomery police arrested King, along with his wife, Coretta. While the Kings were in jail, their house was destroyed by a bomb. Other boycott organizers immediately telephoned Thurgood Marshall in New York, asking for help with King's defense.

Rosa Parks is fingerprinted after her arrest for disobeying a Montgomery, Alabama, segregation law in 1955.

Boycott:
A refusal to buy services or goods in order to change unacceptable policies or conditions.

Ordinances:
Local laws.

The Reverend Martin Luther King Jr.

Thurgood Marshall reads to his son Thurgood Jr. at home in 1958.

Civil disobedience:

Intentionally breaking a law thought to be unfair, usually a law dealing with the rights of individuals.

Acquitted:

Declared innocent of a crime by a court or a jury.

Starting Over

Thurgood was not in New York when the Montgomery bus boycott had begun. He was on his honeymoon in Florida and the Caribbean. In December 1955, Thurgood married Cecilia "Cissy" Suyat, a petite woman of Philippine ancestry who was born on the Hawaiian island of Maui. Cissy had moved to New York in 1947 and had taken a job with the NAACP as a secretary.

By the time Thurgood returned from his trip, the boycott was national news. The NAACP became involved, even though Thurgood opposed boycotts and other actions known as civil disobedience. If there was one thing that defined Thurgood Marshall during his lifetime, it was respect for the law. He always had believed that people should obey laws, even if they disliked them or considered them unfair.

Despite his doubts, Thurgood went to King's defense. Thurgood and his deputy counsel, Robert Carter, challenged the Montgomery segregation ordinance that had led to the arrest of both King and Rosa Parks. A three-judge panel of the federal court supported them, agreeing with the Supreme Court's *Brown* decision. The city of Montgomery appealed, but the Supreme Court declared that segregated seating on buses violated the 14th Amendment. Martin Luther King Jr. was acquitted and Rosa Parks was free to sit in any seat on the city's buses. It was King, however, who became the first African-American passenger on Montgomery's newly integrated bus system.

Thurgood knew the fight against segregation was far from over, but he began devoting more time to his private life. In August 1956, his first son, Thurgood Marshall Jr., was born. Thurgood Sr. was happier than he had been in years. He enjoyed his favorite activities—late-night parties, telling jokes, listening to loud music, and playing with a model railroad that friends had given him. As soon as his son was old enough, he would have someone to share his hobby. And he could tell Thurgood Jr. all about the adventures he and his father, William, had on the railroad years ago as dining car waiters.

Courage in Little Rock

Backed by a growing list of Supreme Court decisions outlawing segregation, African Americans stepped up their protests in the South. As their peaceful demonstrations were met with violence, the entire nation watched the electrifying news reports on television. One of the most dramatic showdowns involved the desegregation of Central High School in Little Rock, Arkansas.

In September 1957, 15-year-old Melba Pattillo volunteered to be one of the first black students to integrate the all-white school. Her parents reluctantly agreed, but they had good reason to be fearful. On the first day of school, a mob of angry whites confronted the nine black students, forcing them away from the building. Days of rioting followed, with gangs of whites driving through black neighborhoods, throwing rocks through windows and yelling hateful words.

Thurgood Marshall meets with the first black students at Central High School in Little Rock, Arkansas, and their NAACP adviser, Daisy Bates.

Orval E. Faubus, Democratic governor of Arkansas.

U.S. Army troops escort black students to school in Little Rock, Arkansas, in 1957.

NAACP lawyer Constance B. Motley and colleagues read the headlines for June 5, 1959, reporting school segregation illegal in Atlanta, Georgia.

The segregationists had a powerful ally. Arkansas governor Orval Faubus led the fight against school integration. He ordered the state's National Guard troops to surround Central High School and keep out any black students who tried to enter.

Thurgood Marshall and the NAACP represented the nine black students. Thurgood got a federal court order to allow the students to attend Central High School. The state quickly appealed, and the case moved to the U.S. Supreme Court. There Thurgood demanded:

> *There must be a definitive action, so that in Arkansas there will be no doubt that the orders of the court cannot be interfered with . . . by . . . mob action.*

Governor Faubus had threatened to close all of the schools in Little Rock if the Court forced the schools to integrate. Thurgood responded: "When a bank is robbed, you don't close the bank. You put the robber in jail."

The Supreme Court ruled against the state, but the crisis did not end. The violence and hatred directed against the black teenagers was shocking. In one of the most dramatic confrontations of the civil-rights era, President Dwight D. Eisenhower ordered thousands of federal troops into Little Rock. The soldiers marched into the city with their rifles drawn. It was an amazing show of force. Nothing like it had been seen since the Civil War. As Melba Pattillo said later:

The troops were wonderful. I went in not through the side doors but up the front stairs, and there was a feeling of pride and hope that yes, this is the United States; yes, there is a reason I salute the flag; and it's going to be okay.

Illustration of Thurgood Marshall on the cover of *Time* magazine, September 1955.

Kennedy's Problem

In 1960, at the height of the civil-rights movement, 43-year-old John F. Kennedy was elected president of the United States—the youngest person ever to hold that office. Kennedy had a problem. He sympathized with African Americans and wanted to show them some support. At the same time, he did not want to offend the powerful southern Democrats who dominated Congress. Those lawmakers—many of whom opposed civil-rights laws—could block any new programs the young president proposed.

Robert F. Kennedy, the president's brother, had an idea that might help. Robert was attorney general of the United States. In that office, he recommended to the president the people he could nominate to serve as federal judges. Robert Kennedy told the president to nominate Thurgood Marshall as a district court judge.

Thurgood seemed to be the perfect choice. He was the best-known civil-rights lawyer in the nation, he was highly respected by many whites, and he was a hero to almost all blacks. In the aftermath of the *Brown* decision, he had earned the nickname Mr. Civil Rights. But when Thurgood heard that he might be nominated for a federal judge's chair, he had other ideas.

Attorney general:
The top law officer of the United States or of a state.

Nominate:
Name someone to be considered for an office or position.

President John F. Kennedy.

Attorney General Robert F. Kennedy, brother of President John F. Kennedy.

Circuit:

A division of the United States, or a state, that is served by a certain court or set of judges.

Chief appeals court judge J. Edward Lumbard swears in Thurgood Marshall as a federal judge in 1961.

The federal court system has three levels. District courts are the lowest. They have juries to hear criminal and civil trials. The courts of appeals are next. They hear appeals from district court decisions. They are made up of panels of judges. The U.S. Supreme Court, with its nine-judge panel, is the highest court in the land.

Although Thurgood had experience in all three courts, he decided that he did not have the patience or the desire to be a trial court judge. He also knew that a Supreme Court appointment was out of the question. Thurgood decided that only the courts of appeals could draw him away from his job with the NAACP. In particular, he wanted to be appointed to the second circuit, which includes New York City. Thurgood and his family would not have to move. That appointment would allow him to spend more time with his wife and sons. His younger son, John William, had been born in 1958.

In May 1961, Robert Kennedy met with Thurgood to discuss the appointment. He heard about Thurgood's preference, but the young attorney general made it clear that a district court job was all he could offer. "You don't seem to understand. It's this or nothing," he said. Thurgood looked squarely at Kennedy and responded:

> *The trouble is that you are different from me. You don't know what it means, but all I've had in my life is nothing. It's not new to me. So good-bye.*

When Thurgood abruptly left the meeting, Robert Kennedy was convinced of his seriousness. He recommended Thurgood's nomination and worked with reluctant members of Congress to win their support. In October 1961, Thurgood Marshall was sworn in as the first African-American judge on the U.S. Court of Appeals for the Second Circuit.

Back to Washington

If Thurgood expected to have a long and quiet career as a court of appeals judge, he was mistaken. In July 1965, three and a half years after his appointment, he was enjoying lunch with friends at a New York City restaurant when he was interrupted by a phone call from one of his law clerks. The clerk stammered that the president had called. Thurgood, annoyed at the interruption, asked, "President of what?" The clerk explained that President Lyndon B. Johnson was calling. But Thurgood calmly went back to his table and finished his lunch. He returned the president's call when he arrived back at his judge's chambers.

President Johnson told Thurgood that he wanted him to replace Archibald Cox, who was resigning from his position as solicitor general. Cox wanted to return to his teaching position at Harvard University Law School.

Thurgood thought about the offer. If he accepted, he would be giving up a lifetime appointment on the appeals court in New York for a job in Washington that, at best, would last only as long as Johnson remained in office. But Thurgood could not resist a challenge. As he later recalled:

Thurgood Marshall, in his solicitor general's cutaway coat, with U.S. Attorney General Nicholas Katzenbach.

I was reluctant at first. But when the President was through with me, I was ashamed I hadn't volunteered. I told [my wife] Cissy that it would call for some belt-tightening, that it might mean she couldn't get a new dress for a year.

Mrs. Marshall's response was, "So?" And when Thurgood told his young sons that they would have to cut back, too, they were only interested in seeing their father in a cutaway—the formal black coat with long tails worn by the solicitor general, along with a pearl gray vest, striped tie, and gray pants.

The solicitor general of the United States represents the federal government in the Supreme Court. And the Court often seeks the solicitor general's views on cases the justices are considering. Because of this special relationship, the solicitor is known in legal circles as the tenth justice. The job was just too interesting for Thurgood to turn down, so he packed up his family and moved to Washington, D.C.

Thurgood quickly settled into the job. He had practiced law before the Supreme Court for years, so he was comfortable there. When Court was in session, the justices always addressed him respectfully as "Mr. Solicitor." In private, however, everyone knew him as Thurgood, the great storyteller who always told a good joke and enjoyed a good party.

A younger Thurgood Marshall laughs with his top aide, Robert Carter, at an NAACP meeting in Atlanta, Georgia, in 1955.

The President Calls Again

In June 1967, the White House placed another call to the Marshall family. This time, Thurgood was with President Johnson in the Oval Office. Cissy Marshall answered the phone. "Take a deep breath and sit down slowly," Thurgood said to her. He handed the phone to the president, who told Cissy that he was going to nominate her husband to the U.S. Supreme Court. Cissy was so elated that she could barely respond. "Thank you so much for having faith in my husband," she replied, as calmly as she could. On August 30, 1967, the U.S. Senate confirmed Thurgood Marshall's nomination to the Supreme Court. He was the first African American to hold that office. A few years later, Lyndon Johnson said of his appointment:

> *When I appointed Thurgood Marshall to the Supreme Court, I figured he'd be a great example to younger kids. . . . All over America that day, . . . thousands of mothers looked across the breakfast table and said: "Now maybe this will happen to my child someday." I bet from one coast to the other there was a rash of new mothers naming their newborn sons Thurgood.*

Thurgood Marshall's wife, Cissy, helps him with his new Supreme Court justice's robe on October 2, 1967.

The Supreme Court of the United States, Washington, D.C.

Photo courtesy of Library of Congress.

Mr. *Justice*

Marshall

Epilogue   1967-1993

Key Events in Thurgood Marshall's Life

Key Events Around the World

1965

1967

The Senate confirms Thurgood's appointment to the Supreme Court on August 30. He is sworn in as the first African-American justice on September 1.

1968

1969

Robert F. Kennedy is assassinated in Los Angeles and Martin Luther King Jr. is assassinated in Memphis, Tennessee.

Thurgood writes the Supreme Court opinion in a case that gives defendants more protection in all of the nation's courts.

1970

Astronaut Neil Armstrong is the first person to walk on the moon.

With Thurgood Marshall's influence, the Supreme Court declares busing can be used to enforce desegregation of public schools.

1972

The first Earth Day is observed to bring attention to the environment.

Thurgood leads the Supreme Court in a decision to overturn the use of the death penalty.

1974

1975

President Nixon resigns from office, following threats of impeachment. Hank Aaron of the Atlanta Braves breaks Babe Ruth's home run record.

1977

The United States withdraws all armed forces from South Vietnam.

Thurgood gets the Supreme Court to uphold the concept of affirmative action to create educational and job opportunities for minorities.

1978

President Carter declares an energy crisis. Gasoline supplies are controlled by the government.

1980

1981

President Reagan stops the use of school busing to end desegregation of public schools and begins to argue against affirmative action.

1983

Martin Luther King Jr.'s birthday is declared a federal holiday.

1985

1986

The NAACP moves its headquarters from New York City to Baltimore, Maryland.

1990

1991

Thurgood Marshall retires from the Supreme Court at age 82.

President Bush appoints Clarence Thomas to take Thurgood Marshall's seat on the Supreme Court.

Justice Marshall dies on January 24.

1993

When Thurgood Marshall was sworn in as an associate justice of the U.S. Supreme Court on September 1, 1967, the Reverend Martin Luther King Jr. hailed his appointment as a "momentous step toward a color-blind society." That's exactly what it turned out to be. During his 24 years on the Supreme Court, he fought a constant battle against racial discrimination.

Thurgood understood that changing racial attitudes sometimes required sweeping action. In 1972, in a case called *Furman v. Georgia*, Thurgood persuaded four other justices to vote to end capital punishment in America. He had opposed the death penalty ever since he first lost a case that resulted in the execution of his client.

Thurgood knew that the death penalty was applied unfairly. Many more minorities were put to death than whites. He considered the death penalty a form of "cruel and unusual punishment," something forbidden by the Constitution's Eighth Amendment:

> *In recognizing the humanity of our fellow human beings, we pay ourselves the highest tribute. We . . . join the approximately 70 other [nations] in the world which celebrate their regard for civilization . . . by shunning capital punishment.*

Although this decision would be reversed later, it had a lasting positive effect. Many states adopted new laws to prevent capital punishment from being applied unfairly to minorities. Thurgood's brief victory had balanced the scales of justice. *Furman v. Georgia* helped protect people who were unable to defend themselves.

Capital punishment:
A court order putting to death a person who was convicted of a crime.

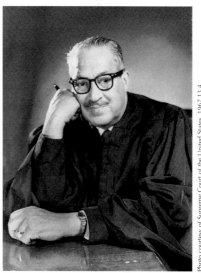

Supreme Court justice Thurgood Marshall.

Students at Central High School in Little Rock, Arkansas, in 1961.

Despite his deep respect for individual rights, Thurgood Marshall believed in powerful government action to integrate the nation's schools. White parents were leaving cities in order to avoid sending their children to schools with black children. In 1970, Thurgood wrote the Court's unanimous decision in *Swann v. Charlotte-Mecklenburg.* The Court ordered school systems to bus students to balance racial enrollments.

Although the decision angered many parents, an entire generation of students learned how to respect and appreciate children of all races. Old barriers that had separated black and white children finally were ending.

Thurgood Marshall also believed in strong action to undo the effects of past injustices. That was his position in *Bakke v. University of California.* Allan Bakke, a white man, had sued the university for rejecting his application to medical school. Instead, the university accepted minority students with lower grades than Bakke.

Thurgood won a partial—but important—victory in the 1978 decision. Although the Court supported Bakke's lawsuit, it also ruled that schools could consider race as a factor in applications. As the Court's opinion stated, "in order to get beyond racism, we must take account of race. There is no other way."

The *Bakke* decision paved the way for affirmative action programs all over America. As a result, thousands more minority students were able to attend colleges and universities. They also had opportunities for better jobs—positions that once were open only to whites.

In these, and many other decisions, Thurgood Marshall served as the conscience of the Court. His personal stories helped the other justices to see the world through *his* eyes. As Justice Anthony Kennedy wrote:

> *His compassion and his philosophy flow from a life and legend*
> *of struggle. His gift of storytelling is not some [minor part] of*
> *Thurgood's character and personality. It is an essential part of*
> *his professional greatness.*

Among the justices, only Thurgood Marshall endured the pain of discrimination. He alone had defended a client in a death penalty case. He alone had escaped from an angry mob. And he alone had visited hundreds of small towns, staying in private homes, sharing simple meals with ordinary people and listening to their hopes and dreams for a better life.

As long as he served on the Supreme Court, Thurgood never forgot those lessons. He also remembered what he had learned when he began memorizing the U.S. Constitution in his high-school basement—that the ideals of the Constitution were real, and not merely words on a page.

In June 1991, when Thurgood retired, a reporter asked him if he thought he had helped the lives of African Americans. He replied, "I think my being on the Court has helped the lives of *all* Americans."

Thurgood Marshall died on January 24, 1993, at the age of 84. More than 18,000 people walked quietly past his coffin in the Great Hall of the Supreme Court Building. Chief Justice William Rehnquist, speaking at the funeral, reminded his listeners about the words carved above the entrance to the Court—"Equal Justice Under Law." Rehnquist said, "Surely no one individual did more to make these words a reality than Thurgood Marshall."

The spirited child from Baltimore had made an impact on justice that his nation never would forget.

After his death, citizens pay their respects to Justice Thurgood Marshall in the Great Hall of the Supreme Court on January 27, 1993.

Acknowledgments

The editors wish to thank the following individuals for their valuable assistance in the preparation of this book:

Leland Ware Jr.

Hon. William H. Murphy Sr.

James P. Turner, formerly of the Civil Rights Division of the U.S. Department of Justice

Robert Moss, photographer

The staff of the Maryland African American Collection of the Enoch Pratt Library, Baltimore, Maryland

Mary Ternes of the Martin Luther King Library, Washington, D.C.

The staff of the Prints and Photographs Division of the Library of Congress

The staff of the National Archives, Washington, D.C.

The staff of the Maryland State Archives, Annapolis, Maryland

Patricia Bracey, Executive Assistant to the Secretary of the Maryland Department on Aging

Banneker-Douglass Museum of Afro-American Life and History, Annapolis, Maryland

The Columbia University Oral History Project

Arleigh Prelow, InSpirit Communications

Bibliography

Ball, Howard. *A Defiant Life: Thurgood Marshall and the Persistence of Racism in America.* New York: Crown, 1998.

Davis, Michael D., and Hunter R. Clark. *Thurgood Marshall: Warrior at the Bar, Rebel on the Bench.* New York: Carol Publishing Group, 1992.

Goodwin, Doris Kearns. *Lyndon Johnson and the American Dream.* New York: St. Martin's Press, 1976.

Hakim, Joy. *All the People (A History of Us, Book Ten).* New York: Oxford University Press, 1995.

Houston, Charles. "The Need for Negro Lawyers," *Journal of Negro Education,* vol. 4, 1935.

———. "Saving the World for Democracy," *Pittsburgh Courier,* August 24, 1940.

———. "The Highway," Baltimore *Afro-American,* 1947.

Kennedy, Anthony M. "The Voice of Thurgood Marshall." *Stanford Law Review,* no. 44 (Summer 1992).

Marshall, Thurgood. Brief before the U.S. Supreme Court in *Shelley v. Kraemer,* 1948.

———. *Columbia University Oral History Project,* New York, February 15, 1977.

———. *Newsweek,* June 26, 1967.

———. *Time,* September 19, 1955.

———. *Time,* September 8, 1958.

———. Oral argument before the U.S. Supreme Court in *Brown v. Board of Education,* 1953.

———. Oral argument before the U. S. Supreme Court in the *Restrictive Covenants Cases,* 1948.

Perlman, Philip. Oral argument in the *Restrictive Covenants Cases,* 1948.

Poling, James. "Thurgood Marshall and the Fourteenth Amendment," *Collier's,* February 23, 1952.

Ross, Irwin. "Thurgood Marshall," Baltimore *Afro-American,* August 20, 1960.

Rowan, Carl. *Dream Makers, Dream Breakers: The World of Justice Thurgood Marshall.* New York: Little, Brown, 1994.

United States District Court for the District of Kansas. Opinion in *Brown v. Board of Education,* 1951.

United States Supreme Court. Ruling in *Brown v. Board of Education,* 1954.

United States Supreme Court. Ruling in *Furman v. Georgia,* 1972.

United States Supreme Court. Ruling in *McLaurin v. Oklahoma State Regents for Higher Education,* 1950.

United States Supreme Court. Ruling in *Sweatt v. Painter,* 1950.

Williams, Juan. *Thurgood Marshall: American Revolutionary.* New York: Times Books, 1998.

Sources for Quotations

The following sources provided the quotations in this book:

Chapter 1:

"Way back before the Civil War"
   Time, September 19, 1955, p. 24

"I can still see Thurgood"
   Davis and Clark, *Thurgood Marshall,* p. 36

"He mentioned the fact that"
   Columbia University Oral History Project, part 1, p. 2

"We lived on a respectable street"
   Davis and Clark, *Thurgood Marshall,* p. 37

Chapter 2:

"The first day, I was given a white coat"
   Time, 1955, p. 24

"We'd argue about everything"
   Newsweek, June 26, 1967, p. 35

"five out of seven nights at the dinner table"
   Columbia University Oral History Project, part 1, p. 5

Chapter 3:

"I made up my mind that I would never get caught again"
   Pittsburgh Courier, August 24, 1940

"If a Negro law school is to make its full contribution"
   Journal of Negro Education, vol. 4, p. 52

"I heard law books were to dig in, so I dug deep"
   Collier's, February 23, 1952, p. 31

"I had to commute from"
   Columbia University Oral History Project, part 1, p. 6

"My first year I lost thirty pounds"
   Williams, *Thurgood Marshall,* p. 56

Chapter 4:

"I don't know anything I did"
   Columbia University Oral History Project, part 1, p. 10

"Once in a while I got a good fee"
   Baltimore *Afro-American,* August 20, 1960, p. 5

"He would say that, with very few exceptions"
   Columbia University Oral History Project, part 1, p. 19

"The kid did not even take the peeling off"
   Williams, *Thurgood Marshall,* p. 60

Chapter 5:

"After a couple of years"
   Columbia University Oral History Project, part 1, p. 22

"He told me to blow my breath in his face"
   Columbia University Oral History Project, part 1, p. 33

Chapter 6:

"This case is not a matter of"

    Marshall, *Restrictive Covenants Cases*

"We all worried about this guy"

    Williams, *Thurgood Marshall*, p. 150

"Attempts are made by such devices"

    Baltimore *Afro-American*, January 24, 1948, p. 1

Chapter 7:

"While it was true that a lot of us might die"

    Time, September 19, 1955, p. 26

"The University of Texas Law School possesses"

    U.S. Supreme Court, *Sweatt v. Painter*

"[The university] handicapped [McLaurin]"

    U.S. Supreme Court, *McLaurin v. Oklahoma State Regents*

"The NAACP is making a direct"

    Houston, Baltimore *Afro-American*, "The Highway," 1947

"Neither Congress nor anyone else can say"

    Rowan, *Dream Makers*, p. 153

Chapter 8:

"Segregation of white and colored children"

    U.S. District Court (Kansas), *Brown v. Board of Education*

Chapter 9:

"Exactly correct"

    Marshall, *Brown v. Board of Education*

"The only way that this Court can decide"

    Marshall, *Brown v. Board of Education*

"Segregation of children in public schools"

    U.S. Supreme Court, *Brown v. Board of Education*

"I think that, even in the most prejudiced communities"

    Davis and Clark, *Thurgood Marshall*, p. 179

Chapter 10:

"I know in the South"

    Marshall, *Brown v. Board of Education*

"There must be a definitive action"

    Time, September 8, 1958, p. 14

"The troops were wonderful"

    Hakim, *All the People*, p. 87

"The trouble is that you are different from me"

    Davis and Clark, *Thurgood Marshall*, p. 224

"I was reluctant at first"

    Davis and Clark, *Thurgood Marshall*, p. 245

"When I appointed Thurgood Marshall"

    Davis and Clark, *Thurgood Marshall*, p. 271

Epilogue:

"In recognizing the humanity of"

    U.S. Supreme Court, *Furman v. Georgia*

"His compassion and his philosophy"

    Kennedy, *Stanford Law Review*, p. 1221

Additional Photo Credits

Index

O

Overturn: definition, 84
Owens, Jesse, *68*
Oxford (Pennsylvania): Lincoln University, *24-26,* 29; public square, *29*

P

Parks, Rosa, *101*-102
Pattillo, Melba, 103; quoted, 104-105
Pearson, Raymond A., *45*
Perlman, Philip: on restrictive covenants, 64
Pilots, black fighter pilots, *67*
Plaintiff: definition, 43
Plessy, Homer, 21
Plessy v. Ferguson, 21-22, 73-74, 80
Police harassment, 10, 56
Precedent: definition, 50
Primary election: definition, 54
Prince Edward County (Virginia) high-school case, *82*
Princess Anne Academy, *44*
Protests: against Jim Crow laws, *64;* against separate but equal rule in schools, *72, 82;* against shooting of a black man by police, *13;* by whites against desegregation, *60-61, 70,* 103-105
Psychological effects of segregation on black children, 84-85
Psychology: definition, 84
Public square: Oxford (Pennsylvania), *29*

R

Racial discrimination: definition, 32. *See also* Civil rights; Racism; Segregation
Racial prestige: definition, 93
Racism: in death penalty, 113; in Thurgood's childhood, 9-10; in the U.S. Army, 31. *See also* Bigots; Racial discrimination
Railroad, model, 103

Railroad workers, *16, 22,* 103
Rebuttal: definition, 91
Reconstruction: definition, 92
Redding, Louis, *100*
Rehnquist, William: quoted, 115
Restrictive convenants, 59-60
Restrictive covenants cases, 61-64, *63*
Reverse: definition, 80
Riots against school desegregation, 103-105
Robinson, Spottswood, *82, 92*

S

Schools: desegregation, 99-100, 103-105, *114;* equal-schools campaign, 41-46; Frederick Douglass High School, *15,* 20; inequality of black and white schools, 20, 42-43, 51, 69-70, 71-72, 74-76, 80-82; Lincoln University, *24-26,* 29; rural schools for black children, *20, 42-43, 81;* segregation in, *20,* 29, 41-46, *42,* 49-50, 67-76, *73,* 80-86, 89-95; segregation protests, *72,* 103-105; in the South, 20, 42-46, *42,* 80-82, *81. See also* Law schools; Teachers
Segregation, 19-22, *19-20;* definition, 10; on buses, 55, 101-102; desegregate (definition), 80; "equal but separate," 21-22, 41, 50, 71-76, *72, 73,* 94; Fourteenth Amendment violation by, 32, 41, 69, 74-76, 90-94, 102; in hospitals, 51; housing discrimination, 59-64; Jim Crow laws, 20-22, 41, *64,* 80; Kansas court statement on, 84; in law practices, 32; in movie theaters, *20, 29;* NAACP antisegregation campaign, 40-46, 49-53, 59-64, 67-76, 80-86, *86;* psychological effects on black children, 84-85; in schools, 20, *20,* 29, 30, 41-46, *42,* 49-50, 67-76, *73,* 80-86, 89-95; Supreme Court decisions on, 21-22, 80-95; Thurgood's decision to fight, 25, 29; on trains, 21, 54. *See also* Civil rights; Integration; Racism
Separate but equal, 21-22, 41, 50, 71-76, *72, 73,* 94

Settlement: definition, 53
Shelley v. Kraemer, 61-64
Shoeshine stand (Harlem), *39*
Sipuel, Ada, *69;* case against the University of Oklahoma College of Law, 68-70, 74
Slave: enslaved (definition), 12; escaped, *11*
Smith v. Allwright, 54
Solicitor general, 108; definition, 64; Thurgood Marshall as, *107*-108
Sousa (Washington, D.C.) Junior High School case, 81
Speaking tours, 52-53
Spectators for Supreme Court trial, *89, 92,* 94
State's attorney: definition, 15
"Straw man," 60-61
Streetcars on Howard Street (Baltimore, Maryland), *9*
Streetcar terminal, *19*
Street scenes, *15, 29;* Baltimore, *9, 13-14;* Chicago, *60;* Harlem, *39, 52;* Yonkers, *59*
Strike: definition, 82; by Prince Edward County high-school students, *82*
Sued: definition, 21
Supremacy: definition, 92
Supreme Court, *89-90, 110; Brown v. Board of Education of Topeka* case, 89-95, *89, 91-92, 94-95;* desegregation ruling, 104; Gaines case against the University of Missouri ruling, 50; mother and child on Supreme Court steps, *95;* 1936 members, *50; Plessy v. Ferguson* ruling, 21-22, 73-74, 80; segregation decisions, 21-22, 80-95; U.S. court system role, 96
Supreme Court justice, Thurgood Marshall as, *10, 109,* 113-115, *113*
Suyat, Cecilia. *See* Marshall, Cecilia
Swann v. Charlotte-Mecklenburg, 114
Sweatt, Heman Marion: case against the University of Texas School of Law, 71-76, *71*

TIME LIFE EDUCATION Time Life Education Inc. is a division of Time Life Inc.

TIME LIFE INC.
PRESIDENT AND CEO: George Artandi

TIME LIFE EDUCATION INC.
PRESIDENT: Mary Davis Holt

Time-Life History Makers
THURGOOD MARSHALL: FREEDOM'S DEFENDER

Managing Editor: Mary J. Wright
Series Editor: Bonnie H. Hobson
Editorial Director: Phillip J. Berardelli

Research and Writing: Leland Ware
  Leland Ware is a professor at St. Louis University School of Law. He is a graduate of Fisk University and Boston College Law School. He is a former counsel for Howard University. He was a trial attorney for the U.S. Department of Justice, Civil Division, and for the U.S. Department of Health, Education, and Welfare. Professor Ware also has practiced law with a private firm in Atlanta, Georgia. He has made several presentations on race and equality issues in the United States and Europe.

Special Editorial Consultant: Juan Williams, author of *Thurgood Marshall: American Revolutionary*

Research Consultant: Ben F. Collins

Text Editors: Patricia Daniels, Allan Fallow, Melva L. Ware
Picture Research: Joan Marie Mathys
Associate Editors/Research and Writing: Laura Heinle, Betsy Thompson
Picture Associate: Angela Bailey
Editorial Assistant: Maria Washington
Technical Art Specialist: John Drummond
Designer: Susan Angrisani, Designsmith, Inc.
Senior Copyeditor: Judith Klein
Correspondent: Christina Lieberman (New York)

Prepress service by the Time-Life Imaging Department

Vice President of Marketing and Publisher: Rosalyn McPherson Perkins
Vice President of Book Production: Patricia Pascale
Director of Book Production: Marjann Caldwell
Director of Publishing Technology: Betsi McGrath
Director of Photography and Research: John Conrad Weiser
Production Manager: Carolyn Bounds
Director of Quality Assurance: James King
Chief Librarian: Louise D. Forstall

First printing. Printed in U.S.A.
School and library distribution by Time-Life Education, P.O. Box 85026, Richmond, Virginia 23285-5026.
Telephone: 1-800-449-2010
Internet: www.timelifeedu.com

TIME-LIFE is a trademark of Time Warner Inc. and affiliated companies

Library of Congress Cataloging-in-Publication Data
Ware, Leland, 1948–
    Thurgood Marshall : freedom's defender / Leland Ware.
      p. cm.—(Time-Life history makers)
    Includes bibliographical references and index.
    Summary: Discusses the life and times of the first African American to serve as a judge on the United States Supreme Court.
    ISBN 0-7835-5449-4
    1. Marshall, Thurgood, 1908-1993—Juvenile literature. 2. Afro-American judges—United States—Biography Juvenile literature. 3. United States. Supreme Court—Biography Juvenile literature.
    [1. Marshall, Thurgood, 1908-1993. 2. Lawyers. 3. Judges. 4. Afro-Americans Biography.] I. Title. II. Series.
KF8745.M34W37   1999
347.73'2634—dc21   99-3971
[b]   CI

We the People of the United States, in Order to form a more perfect Union, establish Justice, insure d

We the People of the United States, in Order to form a more perfect Union, establish Justice, insure dome

Liberty to ourselves and our Posterity, do ordain and establish this Constitution for the United States o

Liberty to ourselves and our Posterity, do ordain and establish this Constitution for the United States of

United States, which shall consist of a Senate and House of Representatives. Section. 2. The House

United States, which shall consist of a Senate and House of Representatives.   Section. 2. The House of R

and the Electors in each State shall have the Qualifications requisite for Electors of the most numerous

and the Electors in each State shall have the Qualifications requisite for Electors of the most numerous B

Age of twenty five Years, and been seven Years a Citizen of the United States, and who shall not, when

Age of twenty five Years, and been seven Years a Citizen of the United States, and who shall not, when ei

apportioned among the several States which may be included within this Union, according to their respect

apportioned among the several States which may be included within this Union, according to their respect

to Service for a Term of Years, and excluding Indians not taxed, three fifths of all other Persons (mod

to Service for a Term of Years, and excluding Indians not taxed, three fifths of all other Persons (modified

of the Congress of the United States, and within every subsequent Term of ten Years, in such Manner a

of the Congress of the United States, and within every subsequent Term of ten Years, in such Manner as

each State shall have at Least one Representative; and until such enumeration shall be made, the Stat

each State shall have at Least one Representative; and until such enumeration shall be made, the State o

Plantations one, Connecticut five, New-York six, New Jersey four, Pennsylvania eight, Delaware one

Plantations one, Connecticut five, New-York six, New Jersey four, Pennsylvania eight, Delaware one, Mar